Hard-Rock, High-Grading and Harlots

Tales of Nevada County in the Days of Gold

By

Brad Prowse

ISBN: 0-7596-9855-4 (Electronic)
ISBN: 0-7596-9856-2 (Softcover)

This book is printed on acid free paper.

1stBooks – rev. 7/30/02

Cover Photo: The Rowe Shaft at Empire Mine State Park in Grass Valley

TABLE OF CONTENTS

PREFACE

The following book is a compilation of articles I have written on the—mostly—early days of Nevada County.

A Hayward, California boy myself, I remember that town before the freeways and developers, when it was small and bucolic. I moved to Nevada County in 1966 to allow my children to experience much the same atmosphere. Struck by the historical richness of the place, I have been writing of her over the past thirty years.

FOREWORD

This tome starts out with a piece written for the GRASS VALLEY UNION newspaper to celebrate the 100th year of Grass Valley's formal (incorporated) existence. It will give you a good feel for the development of the area over the years.

The other articles are a hodgepodge of stories about Nevada County. Between the various chapters, I have included samples from a monthly article I write for the UNION. These were gleaned from the UNION archives of 100 years ago and now deposited in the Nevada County Historical Society's Nevada City library. You may find these 'vignettes' of Nevada County circa 1896—1910 amusing. It's what our ancestors were interested in and its surprising how cosmopolitan Nevada County was, considering its remoteness.

PHOTO CREDITS

Early-day Grass Valley

GRASS VALLEY—ONE HUNDRED YEARS

1893—1993

PART ONE

Brad Prowse

GRASS VALLEY CENTENNIAL-1893-1913

The Passing Of The Frontier

The town of Grass Valley—population around 7000—was incorporated in 1893. It did not spring, however, fullblown, from the brow of some mining god. In fact it had been pretty much an established town since the early 1850s' when, according to one story, some animals strayed away from a party of argonauts camped on Steephollow Creek, near the Bear River. As fate would have it, the animals were found a few miles to the west, happily grazing in a grassy swale. The area became settled shortly after and the name `Grass Valley' seemed to come naturally.

In the first decades after incoporation—1893-1913—Grass Valley enjoyed a status somewhere between a town on the edge of the frontier and the more genteel villages in the valleys below. Though attached to the more `civilized' parts of the state by a thin ribbon of steel extending to Colfax, Grass Valley had strong ties to the principal towns and camps in the remote Sierra foothills, still served by stagecoach. It was a time when road agents were a common scourge—indeed, Sheriff Douglass was killed only five miles from Grass Valley in a shootout with two of same in 1896.

Yet Grass Valley had been enjoying electric lights since 1887 and the telephone arrived in the 1893. It was served by four major churches and several fraternal orders—Masons, I.O.O.F, Knights of Pythias, and a miner's union, among others. Classic plays and recitals were regularly advertised in the Grass Valley Union—along with competitions between baseball clubs, something that was almost a passion with the locals. Teams of miners from the various mines held drilling contests. Firemen's balls were regular events, a favorite of a town that had seen several disastrous fires over the years. In fact, belonging to a hose company was on par with being a member of a prestigious lodge. If Grass Valley was still a little rough about the edges, it had developed a thick veneer of civilization.

The town boundaries of the first decade can still be made out today by simply driving around and looking for the older buildings. The downtown consisted of the first two blocks of Mill Street, which butted into Main, forming a `T.' Buildings then continued for a block or so along Main Street.

The residential area stepped its way up the ridge to the west of the downtown area, all the way to Townsend and Pleasant Streets, shouldering up against Lyman Gilmore's property. There the eccentric inventor was just getting a jump on the Wright Brothers by being the first person (maybe) to put a powered, manned, heavier-than-air craft into the skies.

3

From here the town marched south, past St. Joseph's Church to Boston Ravine then followed Empire Street eastward to Pine and Henderson Streets, near today's Memorial Park. From there it swept north, by the Narrow Gauge depot on Bennett Street to stop on another ridge that overlooked the town around Washington and North School Streets.

The town was predominately Anglo-Saxon, excepting a notable 'Chinatown' that extended from Bank Street to Colfax Avenue, its center laying near today's Gold Bowl Bowling Alley. The Cornish miners probably made the largest inpact of any of the town's residences. Originally hailing from Cornwall, England, where they learned their trade in the tin and copper mines, they were at home in Grass Valley's hard-rock quartz.

These 'Cousin Jacks' left the town of Grass Valley three unique legacies. One is the Cornish pastie. (Pass-tee not pace-tee!) This is a 'pocket' of wheat flower crust encasing meat, vegetables and spices, all baked together. (It was an all-in-one lunch for the miner, something like an Army MRE—Meals-Ready- To-Eat—only they really WERE fit to eat and today are the speciality of several Grass Valley restaurants.) Another is the legend of the 'Tommyknocker,' a small, leprechaun-like creature that was the spirit of a departed miner. Their rapping and tapping in the underground chambers of the mines was supposed to be a warning of cave-in, explosion or other danger. The last 'legacy' is the term, 'Cousin Jack.' Every Cornishman had a 'Cousin Jack' back in the old county who would be happy to come and work in the mines at the slightest hint of a foreman's interest in hiring him.

The remoteness of Grass Valley, and the natural clannishness of the miners, helped to make the town insular. Everyone knew everyone—the paper regularly ran a column on what townspersons had traveled where and when they had returned. And It held fast to the memory of its Gold Rush past. However, the day of the lone prospector, making his fortune with pick and pan, rocker and sluice box, had long since vanished. Hardrock mining took wage earners and expensive machinery—and men in the East with heavy gold chains across the fronts of their ample vests to pay for both.

The prosperity of Grass Valley was almost taken for granted, so steady had its financial base become over the years. And that base rested on one great industry—mining—both its strength and its weakness. This wealth supported the store owners and shopkeepers who sold goods to the mines and the miners…as it paid the wages of the miners. Almost all the money that flowed into the town came from mining. What didn't was generated by outlaying agriculture, water canal systems and the lumbering interests.

As the decade swung into the twentieth century the local paper gave up more space to events outside Grass Valley—the Russo-Japanese War, the unrest in Mexico, the conflict with Spain. Though the town continued to concern itself with local issues like the establishment of a free library or the latest `flicker' showing at a downtown auditorium, the new century was making inroads. By 1913 automobile lines running to towns like Alleghany and Downieville had largely replaced the stagecoach. Locally, a person could buy himself an Indian motorcycle for around $250. If the town seemed isolated and inward looking, there were events taking place on the other side of the earth that soon would focus the attention of Grass Valley on the outside world.

Brad Prowse

GRASS VALLEY—ONE HUNDRED YEARS

PART TWO

GRASS VALLEY CENTENNIAL-1913-1933

Years Of Prosperity

Perhaps the thing to note about the affect of the World War on Grass Valley is...it had so little affect! War or no war, the stamp mills continued their steady cadence, the miners went into the earth and the gold kept coming out and into the coffers of the mine owners—minus that amount a clever miner might be able to high-grade...

True, the Northstar had to put a few of their stamps out of production due to the wartime manpower shortage. And the owners found that inflation had pushed production costs perilously close to the going price of gold—a bit over $20 an ounce. Still, they were willing to continue mining and wait out the war, hoping for the resumption of a normal profit-to-cost ratio.

This isn't to say that the town didn't send its share of men off to fight—seventeen would lose their lives on the fields of France in the 'War-To-End-All-Wars.' But, overall, there wasn't much change in the everyday activities of Grass Valley. Though The Union reported in banner headlines on the conflict—and the influenza epidemic that was taking even more lives than the war—the back pages reflected a small town tranquility.

Nor did the arrival of prohibition and the Roaring Twenties do much to shake the town from its steady ways. Thirsty miners weren't to be deterred by a law passed 3000 miles away. In the unincorporated areas people with access to grapes or hops made a little wine or beer to sell to the trustworthy. Even In Grass Valley, should a person become parched, there were spots that served a clear liquid from Mason jars—moonshine. The local law pretty much looked the other way. A person caught running a speakeasy might not face much more than a $150 fine.

The miners lived not by alcohol alone. There was a bordello called 'Mabel's' behind the city hall, on Stewart Street. (The building is still there but today it's a respectable apartment house.) And there was another 'house' across from the city hall on Main Street. (Perhaps this is where the habit of referring to town officials as 'City Fathers' came from...)

But changes there were—particularly as Grass Valley moved into the 1920s.' Many town streets were paved around 1923 as the auto replaced the horse. And, surprisingly, the town—and county—exhibited a downturn in population. Grass Valley had around 8,000 residents in 1895. From 1900 on through the mid-1930s' the population of the town hovered around 4,000. This partly had to do with the industrialization of other areas of California, especially the Bay Area. Nevada County miners were drawn to the new jobs there. They could find work that didn't require them to live their lives in almost perpetual darkness—nighttime when they weren't working, stygian black when they were. Slowly the town was becoming more cosmopolitan. Baseball rivalries continued but there was now a new golf course to tempt the athletic. And The Union headlines reflected an increased interest in international affairs; the Naval Conference in London—the uprising of Ghandi's followers in India—European politics. But mining news could still find a ready place on the front page. Duly noted was the opening of mines such as the Boundary, the Spring Hill and the Allison Ranch. The reopening of the Bullion Shaft or the Northstar's new strike—the comeback of the Idaho-Maryland or the Polar Star. The town knew where its bread and butter came from.

In 1930 Chinatown burned. It was never rebuilt. The inhabitants either left the area or found housing among the general population. It signaled the end of an era of prejudice and xenophobia toward the Chinese that had been a blot on the mining country since the inception of the Gold Rush. From here on, the citizens of Chinese ancestry were pretty much assimilated into the general population of Grass Valley, finally accepted as respected members of the town.

And what of the Great Depression? Like the Great War, it was noted, commented on...and largely ignored. Seemingly, an economic fence had been placed around the county. The miners continued to be employed, the gold seemed inexhaustible and the town prospered. There were at least nine grocery stores, seven clothing stores, four meat markets, three shoe stores, six drug and/or ice cream parlors and two hardware stores in Grass Valley. All would continue to enjoy a robust business if the Grass Valley area mines continued to produce...and produce they did.

In the period from 1918 to 1924 the Empire/Pennsylvania Mines were bringing up $1,500,000 a year in gold. The Northstar did equally well. (Its total production up to 1933 reached $33,000,000.) In the years 1918-1924 the production of all Grass Valley mines totaled $15,000,000. There were 1000 to 1200 men employed in these mines (1924) and the payroll averaged $150,000 a month...almost all pumped back into the local economy. On top of this was the bounty of the harvest; orchards of pears and apples added to the economy of the city. (Later problems—competition from growers in the valley, disinterest, a pear blight—would reduce the value of the county's crops. To date, agriculture has not regained its previous economic importance to Nevada County.)

This isn't to say there weren't unemployed in the county. Several hardscrabble camps sprung up—to note a few, one near the Bridgeport bridge and another near Steephollow Creek, just off U-Bet Road. Here men, mostly refugees from other parts of a depression-wracked America, set to with pan and sluicebox, much as their forefathers had done eighty years before. They tried to glean what flakes or nuggets that may have been missed by their ancestors. However Grass Valley itself escaped the economic ravages besetting the rest of the country—indeed, the world.

In 1933, the end of Grass Valley's fourth decade of incorporation, the Depression was really setting in for the rest of America. Bank failures were becoming rife and the country went off the gold standard. (There was one bright spot—the 18th Amendment was repealed!) But work in the mines was steady. In Grass Valley it seemed as if the turmoil facing the rest of the country didn't matter—that Grass Valley was impervious to outside forces. If so, events were coming to a head half way around the world that would, soon, change the town forever.

GRASS VALLEY—ONE HUNDRED YEARS

PART THREE

GRASS VALLEY CENTENNIAL-1933-1953

Twilight Of The (Mining) Gods

The first years of Grass Valley's fifth decade as an incorporated town were perhaps the high point of hardrock mining in the area. Over 2500 miners were employed in various Nevada County mines and Grass Valley accounted for 1700 of them. This resulted in a payroll of $314,000 a month (1940), most of it spent in the town. Overall, the Grass Valley mines were producing $11,000,000 a year. From 1930 to 1940, the Idaho-Maryland and the Brunswick mines alone brought out $26,700,000 in gold. (During this period, California gold production hit nearly $46,000,000 a year, the highest since 1862 and twice the worth of the petroleum pumped out of the ground.)

And there didn't seem to be any end in sight. The Empire and the Brunswick were both sinking new shafts to follow recently discovered veins of gold. Part of this activity was due to the Roosevelt Administration. It took America off the gold standard in 1934 and forbade the metal from being held by private citizens. Other than jewelry and collectors pieces, all privately held gold had to be turned in. (It was an order that would stand until rescinded by President Ford almost forty years later.) At the same time, gold was pegged at a new price—$35 an ounce. Compared to the old break-even price of $20.67, gold mining was now quite profitable. And some local mines were producing 175 to 200 tons of ore a day. The mighty Idaho-Maryland mine properties brought to the surface up to 600 tons per day.

Grass Valley reflected this prosperity. The town contained 178 stores. (Of that number 25 were food stores, 32, liquor—a disparity, but to show that the townspeople were really a sober lot, over $1,200,000 was spent on food, only $383,000 on booze...) The population, which had dipped below 4000 in the early 1930s,' hit 5700 in 1940. It would not be that high again until the mid-1970s.'

The only dark spot anyone could see—dark if you were a mine owner— was labor unrest. A concerted attempt was made to unionize the mines in 1941. In May of that year this resulted in a 19-day strike against the Idaho-Maryland. It finally ended in a victory for the miners...but the victory was short lived. Other events happening in the world would, seven months later, push labor strife, indeed gold mining itself, into the background—the bombing of Pearl Harbor.

At first the Japanese attack on December 7, 1941, didn't seem to have much direct affect on the town—though it certainly made young, draft-eligible males anxious. A few miners moved out of Grass Valley in response to war-related jobs opening up elsewhere. Still, overall, there wasn't any indication that the mines would have to be shut down. Then, in August of 1942, a few small articles appeared in the Union, hinting that the War Production Board might have to curtail gold and silver mining. Two months later, on October 8, 1942, President Roosevelt issued order L-208. This order closed down, within sixty days, all non-essential civilian work including gold and silver mining. The men and material used to run the mines could be put to better use sustaining the war effort.

The mines were closed. Mine management was allowed a skeleton crew to keep the pumps running—so the mines would remain water-free—and maintain mine machinery. Everyone else was laid off. Some mines still used mules to haul the ore carts. Mines such as the Empire, the Golden Center and the Pennsylvania brought up the animals and turned them out to pasture. (One wonders what the mules thought when they saw the blue sky for the first time. They had spent their lives—born, bred, dying—all underground).

The Nevada County Narrow Gauge Railroad to Colfax was shut down and its rails sold for scrap. The roadbed, no longer thought to be needed, was abandoned. (In hindsight this was a bad decision. What would a present-day Nevada County—a tourist Mecca—give for such an attraction now?)

It was the Government's thought that the miners, set free from digging gold, would be able to work other mines around the country—perhaps in the coal industry. As a matter of fact, most of them left the mines to take up factory or shipyard jobs in the Bay Area. Others found work at rapidly expanding Beale Airbase and like nearby government facilities. Few seem to have ended up still working underground by the war's end. In any case, while suffering a population drop of around 400, Grass Valley continued to enjoy a steady influx of money for its stores and businesses. The town was finding that other sources of income did exist.

With the mines closed news of the war dominated the front pages of the Union—and mining seemed forgotten. But with the coming of the war's end the Government rescinded its order—even questioning if it had been necessary—and the mines were free to open. The machinery was serviced, the hoists were checked out and the stamps set to pounding. Those mines still using mules pulled them from their pastures and consigned them again to a world of perpetual gloom. The Empire, the Idaho-Maryland, the Golden Center and the Pennsylvania were once more ready to wrest gold from the grasp of the stubborn quartz and enrich the town...only now the town really didn't need it.

In the years since the mines had closed the town had found other resources. While the money mining brought in was certainly welcome, it no longer ruled the town's economy as it had prior to the war. This fact would soon become of paramount importance as the end of the town's third score years neared. Grass Valley held only 5000 people while the county population stood at around 20,000 total. But both town and county were poised to undergo a drastic change, though few seemed to realize it. And mining was about to attain the status of legend, just as had the Gold Rush and the `Day's of 49.'

GRASS VALLEY—ONE HUNDRED YEARS

PART FOUR

Brad Prowse

GRASS VALLEY CENTENNIAL-1953-1973

Slumbering Giant

The Grass Valley mines contributed over $300,000,000 to the wealth of California in the over 100 years of their operation...much of this during a time when bread was five or ten cents a loaf. It came to an end in 1957. In that year the Empire Mine closed down, following the closing of the Idaho-Maryland a year earlier. The mine owners threw in the sponge, bowing to the pressures of rising costs, labor unrest and the fixed price of gold. An industry that had, for over 100 years, been the dominant force of the town—the focus of its culture—ceased to exist. The Reign of the Golden Calf had ended. Its going did not destroy the soul of the town but it did cut it adrift—some may question whether it has yet been regained.

But the town, like any organism, had begun, years before, to respond to the change in its fortunes. The emergence of the automobile and the improvement of roads brought a new economic force to Grass Valley. A trickle at first, after WW II more people were coming to the area for recreation. The `flat-lander,' so looked down upon by many of the second, third and fourth-born generations of Grass Valleyites, was becoming a boon to the Sierra towns.

Other economic opportunities were also coming into play. The lumber industry started to expand, opening up labor-intensive jobs, just the ticket for men who were used to hard work. Many a man who had been bucking an airdrill in the Empire or mucking out a shaft in the Brunswick now said he was `going to mine lumber.'

Government jobs became available, either at the burgeoning bases in the valley or with county, state or national park and forest systems. The NID—Nevada Irrigation District—was expanding. It was a maze of more-or-less inter-connected canals, lakes and ponds that had originally been put into existence to feed hydraulic mining. In the years since the big water monitors had been legislated out of business, NID had served mostly surrounding farms and the towns. Now it was getting into the houses put up by subdividers. Service industries sprung up and a few small high-tech manufacturing ventures opened their doors. Even some embryo shopping centers were built.

Also, improved roads and nearby freeways allowed people to drive to the many jobs available in the Sacramento Valley—and, somewhat ominously, opened up Nevada County to an invasion of valley people...not all tourists. Some of these people were coming to stay. NID was more and

21

more being asked to furnish water service to private residents and housing developments in the unincorporated areas.

By 1966 there were 1300 government jobs in the county and 1075 people employed in wholesale and retail trades. There were 900 service jobs and manufacturing employed 425. Mining? Just 25—vs. 2500 thirty years before. (While the threat of public outrage certainly prevents the mines from ever opening again, their specter will forever hover over the town. The gold is still there—in great profusion—and the shafts and tunnels need be but pumped and shored and rugged men—or machines or robots—could be sent down into them once more. Such action might occur if there is some unforeseen economic or social upheaval...like the original Gold Rush was...)

Grass Valley's population continued to decline; in 1960 it held 4,876 residents, about the same as 1900, but changes were coming. Land here was relatively cheap. The air was clear. The climate was mild and the people were friendly—not counting a few hardcore 'Cousin Jacks' who felt that anyone who had been here less than 100 years was a newcomer. People started moving in to stay...

For the most part, the newcomers settled in the yet-sparcely populated unincorporated areas. Some of them lived in new developments built close to town—Starbright Acres, for instance, just past the Fairgrounds. Others lived further away—Lake of the Pines and, later, Lake Wildwood. Many of the new arrivals were retirees—which led to mobile home parks springing up. But there were also young people, looking for inexpensive land where they could build a house and raise a family.

The increased labor pool, cheap land, expanding local infrastructure and desirable living conditions led to even more entrepreneurs—manufacturing, service, retail trades—moving in. It was a snowballing effect—still small but becoming quite noticeable. And Grass Valley was the main place for the newcomers to spend their money.

By the early 1970s' Grass Valley's population—around 5,400—had reached its highest number since the mid-1890s.' The Golden Center Freeway—to some a concrete arrow embedded in the heart of the town, to others a Godsend in relieving traffic—increased the flow into the area and between Grass Valley and its sister town to the north, Nevada City. That town, even more cloistered than Grass Valley had been during its heyday, elected to restrict growth and strictly manage development within its borders. The town would not depend so much on county growth as being a reflection of the past, catering to locals and visitors seeking the aura of a time gone by.

Downtown Grass Valley, however, seemed to dither, unable to decide if it should become a modern shopping center, a jewel-like island of the past or something in between. It made halfhearted and disjointed efforts to recapture the 1870-era facades of its buildings. Often it was individual businessmen or property owners who tried to rescue them from the stuccoed 1920s' attempts to primp for the Twentieth Century.

Finally, it was realized that the town had too many buildings from a later age—1920s' to 1940s'—to really make the transition to a town where every other store was an art gallery and the ones in between cappuccino houses. (Never mind that the thirsty and lusty miners could support a town where every other store was a saloon and those in between were...well, another type of establishment. The miner was gone).

In 1973, at the end of the town's eighth decade, the county was growing rapidly. There were apartment complexes building on what little unused land Grass Valley still held. Ideally, the county planners and town planners should have been working hand-in-glove to settle on a controlled growth policy for the whole county. Whether the growth was just too fast for them, they were overburdened or what, it didn't happen. Growth was allowed to take place haphazardly. The results weren't apparent yet but a four-letter word—mall—would soon provide problems for everyone.

GRASS VALLEY—ONE HUNDRED YEARS

PART FIVE

GRASS VALLEY CENTENNIAL-1973-1993

The Gold Isn't In The Ground...It IS The Ground

If you own a piece of property in Nevada County you probably will find, somewhere in the title description, a clause that states `...all minerals, metal matter...beneath said property...up to 100 feet of the surface...' is reserved to someone else, usually a mining company. The mine owners were willing to sell off the surface ground as long as they had the right to the gold beneath it. They had it wrong...the wealth turned out to be on top.

A house on a half acre near town that sold for $18,000 in 1966 sold for $31,000 eight years later, in 1974. In 1990, just before the recessionary dip of `91-92, the same home was appraised at $175,000. The 1966 price wouldn't make a good down payment on the price 25 years later. Even the land around North San Juan—usually considered inhabited by ex-Hippies, adherents of Zen and people who grow strange, reclusive crops—saw land values increase. It was now being settled by Boomers types, almost—horrors!—bringing respectability to the area. All this was caused by a population explosion that, by 1992 saw the county soar to 84,000 people. Grass Valley had survived fires, depressions, wars, the closing of the mines—could it survive unprecedented growth in the next two decades of its incorporated life?

In 1979 the town had a population of 6,250, a number it hadn't seen since the last century. (By 1990 it would reach 9,400!) It was the largest town in the county and it had a problem. People would speak of `Shopping in Grass Valley,' but they were often referring to the new shopping malls built on the outskirts of town—to the east, Glenbrook Shopping Center and to the west, the K-Mart/Pine Creek Shopping Centers. All are strip malls— long rows of business houses bordered by an expansive parking area. None—as of today, 1993—is within the city boundaries.

What then of Downtown Grass Valley, the traditional hub of the city? The area lost several key business. Pennys moved to the Pine Creek Center while Wards closed up shop. Two large hardware stores, dating back to the last century, moved or shut their doors. Grass Valley can certainly survive without a viable `downtown' shopping area, but lacking it, the town turns into another vague, faceless urban entity. It might start resembling any number of once-small, independent towns along the coast and in the valley, now one seamless, unidentifiable sprawl. The Downtown around Mill and Main was in trouble and the Grass Valley Downtown Business Association took up the challenge.

Though it had lost key stores the town still had a lot going for it. The residential area of Grass Valley—that part of the town within the boundary's of fifty years ago—retains much of its historic flavor. Many older homes built between 1880 and 1920 still sit on town lots. Grass Valley has made a few annexations and some apartment complexes have been built. However, most of the latter are either away from the old parts of town or blend in well enough so that they aren't obtrusive.

Traffic may seem a problem—the two biggest trouble spots are at the confluence of Mill, Main and Auburn Streets and again, two blocks down, at Neal and Auburn. However, compared to the Glenbrook boondoggle, these are relatively minor and limited to the late parts of the afternoon. Further, much of the so called 'parking problem' in the Downtown area is a matter of perception. A customer shopping at a mall will park a distance away from a store, but it seems closer because it can be seen from the car. A Downtown shopper might have to park around the corner from a store but actually have less distance to walk.

The Downtown Association has worked to maintain a balance between 'boutiques' and service business—clothing stores, shoe stores, coffee shops and the like. They are trying hard to make sure Downtown contains a mix of business that will serve the needs of the local community. The Association is purposely shying away from making Grass Valley just a tourist attraction. (The lone super market in the Downtown area—one of Safeway's smallest stores—helps to bring foot traffic to the Downtown area. Should it go, the area probably would be the poorer for its leaving.) So while the town has changed business type to some degree it has not lost businesses. In fact, it presently has only one vacant store. At least one mall has several vacancies.

Downtown, with its slower pace and feeling of 'town,' has much to recommend itself over the malls. Both malls created traffic problems dwarfing Grass Valley's shopping district—problems they have largely left for the taxpayer to correct. And neither was built to take advantage of the natural beauty the area possessed prior to the malls being built. Had they stayed away from their strip-mall design and opted for keeping the trees and topography as it existed, weaving their shops and business among them in a natural setting befitting the Sierras, they would pose an even greater threat to the town. Instead they appear sterile. Only the Downtown provides a feeling that is a throwback to a day when shopping was a leisurely experience, not an endurance race.

A recent report projects a county population of 210,000 by 2010, only seventeen years away. More mall-type development is already proposed for the county. Hopefully, the planning boards of the various governmental entities will jointly look at these plans, cooperating together to determine if Nevada County really needs or wants more development.

In any event, the merchants of Downtown Grass Valley don't intend to let the area die. They will continue working to maintain a business mix that will attract people to the traditional heart of the town. Grass Valley was incorporated in 1893 but it has been around since about 1852. It won't be that easy to kill the old girl off.

ONE HUNDRED YEARS AGO

IN NEVADA COUNTY

APR-1895

by

Brad Prowse

After a wet March, the frosty nights and windy, cold days of April have been refreshing. But by mid-month the farmers welcomed the rain that fell for a few days, stopped and returned at month's end.

The Union has found a new home in the Cox building on the corner of Auburn and Bank Streets.

The vote to build a sewer system for Grass Valley went down the drain, 396 against to 337 for.

Money orders can now be bought—but not cashed—at the French Corral post office.

National Guard Companies D of Auburn and H of Grass Valley held a shooting match, firing .45-70 Springfield rifles at 200 yards. Company H was the winner.

The remains of William Gale, the mail carrier lost in a storm, were recently found near English Mountain Mine. His arm and one hand were missing.

Worthley's Hotel in Washington caught fire but the timely application of a bucket brigade saved the structure.

Virgina City is in the middle of a bicycle craze. In fact, the riding of bicycles is spreading throughout the country, including the local area. Even women are learning to ride, now that the former objection to doing so has been overcome.

And a speedy young woman who struck town a few days ago gave an exhibition on a wheel. She drew such a crowd that the marshall ordered her to desist. She was not wearing bloomers.

The Brunswick Mine has struck a rich ledge at 800 feet.

A well-known colored man, `Bumble-Bee' Hicks, died of a fit while in custody of the county for a mental examination.

A wagonload of wood became stuck on East Broad Street. The wagon was unloaded but it still took eight horses to pull the vehicle free.

Celestials are opening up the old Eastern Mine gravel claim at Hunts Hill.

And two Chinese merchants in Dutch Flat were attacked by highbinders. They were slashed by knives and hatchets and relived of $2000.

A one-legged hobo has been begging on the streets the past couple of days. He no sooner cages a dime then he is off to the nearest saloon—to toast the health of his benefactor, no doubt.

Constable Dillon and two companions left town to search for tramps who are stealing chickens. The two men found a nickel and immediately retired to town to spend it. The tramps escaped.

And in a meeting leading businessmen agreed that a vigilance committee needs to be organized to deal with the hobo problem.

The Union reports that Grass Valley can give no encouragement to laborers. There are already too many unemployed here now.

R. B. Colty, owner of the Spanish Mine, made a wager with James Hennessy that Hennessy could not drive him, using a team, from Grass Valley to Sacramento in four hours. They left at two PM but it's not known if they made it by six.

A troupe of men and women, white, colored and Chinese, held a 'hoola-hoola' and 'muscle' dancing exhibition under a tent near the depot the other night. It was 'men-only' and many bald heads were in evidence. The marshall observed to see that things were kept within limits. When the company appeared in Nevada City, the marshall there threatened to arrest them for putting on an 'immoral' show.

Two-thirds through the month and snow is falling on Washington Ridge. The stage running from Sierraville to Truckee has found the going rough due to rain-sodden snow.

Marshall Getchell and Deputy Sheriff Neagle took five discharged prisoners to Colfax. They were a hard lot and it was thought better they were released to a freight train for pastures new.

A young boy who runs an express team had a runaway that tore down Spring Street, across the suspension bridge and up Piety Hill before stopping. Nothing was left of the wagon but the horses were unhurt.

Milie Christine, the two-headed woman who was at the Mid-Winter Fair, has been booked for Nevada City.

The telephone agent will be along soon to talk subscribers into substituting long distance telephones for the ones they now have.

San Francisco's New Women Club believes that the new woman will be the forerunner of a new and better man. These women evidently have large ideas on the Darwinian plans.

The Nevada County Electric Power Company is proposing to build a plant on the Yuba to supply Grass Valley and Nevada City with electricity. Many mines, closed down because of the cost of steam or water power, will be able to reopen with the less expensive electricity.

An insurance war is sweeping the state, driving prices down 25 to 50 percent.

The Board of Supervisors has abolished the chain gang.

A broken pump in the Maryland Mine has caused the workers to be laid off for the past two weeks.

A local paper claims that shutting down hydraulic mining has cost the country 225 million dollars, all to protect a few potato patches and cabbage fields that could have been bought up for $500,000. Instead, the paper goes on, homes have been broken up, families scattered and men deprived of employment, all to keep a little silt out of the valley.

An item in the Union tells of a Christopher Ritter, who formerly worked at Fords Theater, and his story that he helped John Wilkes Booth, the Lincoln assassin, to escape—that another man was killed in Booth's stead. He claims Booth is still alive in South America, working as an actor.

Shamus O'Brian, a drama, was put on by the James Ward Company at the Nevada Theater.

Lizzie Temby of Grass Valley was severely burned last night when her robe was ignited by a candle.

The Southern Pacific Sunset Limited boasts it can take you from San Francisco to New York in 119 hours. The fastest rail time in this country was made recently between Philadelphia and Atlantic City. It averaged 76.5 miles per hour.

Around the state, nation and world, the Union reports:

The Sacramento and San Francisco papers are putting in type setting machines. Thousands of printers will be put out of work and the country will be flooded with tramp printers.

The grisly murders of two young women, both found within a few days of each other in San Francisco's Emmanuel Baptist Church, are the talk of northern California. Theodore Durrant, a medical student, is suspected of the hideous crimes.

Pugilist Jake Kilrain is preparing for a 25 round match at Coney Island next month.

The Epinal Reservoir in France has burst, taking a hundred lives and flooding a large area.

The Mikado announced the completion of a peace treaty between Japan and China.

The State Department is worried over Great Briton's attempt to acquire territory in Venezuela where both nation's troops threaten war. The British are also engaged in a customs collecting dispute in Nicaragua. It's not unlikely that the U.S. will be drawn into the fray.

Electric Bitters, available for 50 cents a bottle at Carr Brothers Drugstore, will cure all liver and kidney ailments and is also good for pimples, boils, salt rheum, any affliction caused by impure blood and will drive malaria from the system, cure headaches, constipation and indigestion.

TWO GHOSTS, ONE NEAR GHOST

AND TWO RESURRECTED GHOSTS

by

Brad Prowse

In 1848, California's Sierra foothills were one of the most pristine areas on earth. Only a few migrating Indian tribes such as the Miwok and the Miadu occasionally trespassed upon the forest serene. Then came the white man...

Between 1849 and 1851 numerous towns, villages, camps and wide-spots-in-the-road-with-a-name transformed the bucolic tranquility forever as men scraped the earth for its hoard of gold. Many—most—of these sites would disappear as soon as the gold played out, perhaps in only a few months or years. Others would survive and even linger to this day, though only a tenuous shadow of their former selves. And a few would live on in a semblance of permanence.

But the majority did fade away, to leave only interesting sounding place names on maps—You-Bet, Red Dog, Volcano, Hobart Mills. What follows are sketches of five old towns. Two are complete ghosts—Timbuctoo and Cherokee—and barely anything exists to mark their existence. Another, Graniteville, came as close to being ghost as a town can, only to revive somewhat with the suburbia creep to the foothills. And two others, Alleghany and Rough & Ready, never were in danger of going completely away but never have regained their earlier glory, either.

TIMBUCTOO

Timbuctoo, in Yuba County, east of Marysville, was worked by miners as early as 1850. One of the first miners was an escaped slave who had originally been captured in the French Sudan. He claimed his native town was Timbuktu. He made a successful strike there and convinced the other miners to name the town after his birthplace and, with a slightly different spelling, Timbuctoo it became.

Timbuctoo had a post office by 1858, and almost 3500 inhabitants during the heyday of hydraulic mining. The town pumped out $10,000,000 in gold a year and contained many churches, hotels, theaters—and saloons.

The town received a double whammy from a disastrous fire in the 1870s and the Sawyer Decision in 1884 that put a halt to most hydraulic mining. Washing down the mountainsides with huge water cannons—monitors—was causing the valley rivers to silt up, giving the dwellers there flooding problems they live with to this day. The town then faded quickly.

WHAT'S TO SEE: Not a lot—just the tumbled down frame and roof of the Wells-Fargo building built in 1855, some stone walls and a few old wagons.

GETTING THERE: From Marysville, take Highway 20 east about 18 miles. Around a mile after crossing the bridge over the Yuba River, watch for a road sign indicating an intersecting road on the left. Take this road—there should be a 'bridge out 1 mile' warning sign as you enter. The site, surrounded by a chain-link fence, is .8 of a mile further on down a broken up asphalt road.

Starting on Highway 20 at Grass Valley, the distance is about 15 miles. Just past Smartville—an old early-day town in its own right—look for the 'bridge out 1 mile sign' on the right and exit there.

FACILITIES: A grocery store in Smartville and that's about it. The closest gas/food is Penn Valley or Marysville.

TRAVEL TIME: 1.75 hours. (All times approximate and are timed from Sacramento through Grass Valley/Nevada City).

ROUGH & READY

Rough and Ready is located in Nevada County. The town was settled in 1849 by a group of ex-soldiers, the Rough and Ready Company. It was lead by a Captain Townsend who had served under General 'Old Rough and Ready' Taylor in the war with Mexico a few years before. Hence, the town took its name from them.

The town's greatest claim to fame is that it succeeded from the Union in 1850. It seems the miners became irked with the Federal government over law rulings, taxes and such. So they decided to secede, forming the Great Republic of Rough Ready, and sent a proclamation off to Washington to that effect.

The miners waited but no reaction ever came from the East. Finally, with the 4th of July approaching, the miners realized that, as a separate republic, they would have no reason to get blind, stumbling drunk in a patriotic fever over the founding of the United States...so they voted themselves back into the Union and went on a fine toot.

Though the placer deposits were exhausted by 1855, the town continued to grow and once held more than 300 houses. Fire, though, the ban of all gold camps, swept through the town on several occasions.

The town began to languish after the fire of 1859 and the surface gold the town depended on played out. By 1880 there were only around two dozen houses and a single store.

Until about twenty years ago, Rough and Ready consisted of a post office, a grocery store, a cemetery and a few homes. Indeed, the 'downtown' still consists of little more than the post office and grocery, Fippin's blacksmith shop and the old toll house. But in the ensuing years, the surrounding hills have become relatively filled with homes and small ranchos.

WHAT'S TO SEE: There's a few old buildings and a fairly large pioneer cemetery (still active). A flag proclaiming the town as the 'Republic of Rough and Ready' flies on a flagstaff by Fippin's and on the last Sunday of each June Succession Days are held. This is a day filled with music, dancing, skits, old cars, hot dogs and beer.

GETTING THERE: The town is on the Old Rough & Ready Highway, 3 miles west of Grass Valley, or 25 east miles from Marysville on Highway 20 to a left on the Rough & Ready Highway.

FACILITIES: Not much. Gas is available in Grass Valley or Penn Valley. Rough & Ready has only one grocery store but they make a heck of a deli sandwich. Grab a bun, a brew and sit on the covered porch and watch the world go by.

TRAVEL TIME: 1.25 hours.

CHEROKEE

Cherokee is located in Nevada County and was worked early on by a party of Cherokee Indians who prospected in the area around 1850. When a town sprung up a year or two later, and water was brought in by ditches, the town was named Cherokee. By 1852 there were 400 inhabitants. It was said a miner could make $50 a day there, cash in hand.

The town saw its greatest prosperity from the mid-1850s to the mid-1860s and many business were still listed in a directory as late as 1867. The town declined rapidly after that, though there were still around 200 people living in Cherokee in 1880. But the town finally faded away and a religious retreat, the Ananda Community now rests on part of the site.

WHAT'S TO SEE: A handful of old buildings still stand in the general area where Cherokee once thrived. Some look livable, others are obviously abandoned. All are on private property.

GETTING THERE: From Nevada City, drive about 11 miles to Tyler-Foote Road, on the right. From Marysville, it's 25 miles to Pleasant Valley Road in Penn Valley, turn left 15 miles to Tyler-Foote. Then, go down Tyler-Foote Road 4 miles and make a left on Sage Road. Cherokee was located just off Tyler-Foote in this area.

FACILITIES: Gas and food are available at North San Juan, a few miles past Tyler-Foote on Highway 49. Otherwise, it's back to Nevada City or Penn Valley.

TRAVEL TIME: 1.75 hours.

GRANITEVILLE

First settled in 1850 and named Eureka, Graniteville was one of the true High Sierra gold camps, set at around 4900 feet in elevation. At one point, the population reached 1000 souls. Rich placer deposits were exhausted by 1865 but quartz mining took over. In 1867 $20,000,000 in gold was taken out of the nearby mines. That same year, a post office was established in the town, now named Graniteville.

The town remained an important trading place into the 1900s with 30 active mines along with at least one sawmill. In 1906 the local all-grade school held 33 students.

But the area declined as the town moved further into the 20th century, though there still was some mining activity after World War II. By 1923 here were no regular businesses operating and the post office closed in 1959. The final death knell of Graniteville was rung in 1948 when the Gold State Hotel burned down. It had been a summertime mecca for many in the warmer foothills and valley below. Few now bothered to visit the lonely little town near the peak of the Sierras. By the late 1960s there was only one resident who stayed there all year around through Graniteville's sometimes harsh winters.

Today the old gal has perked up a bit with many of the old houses showing signs of new paint and repairs. There are three year-round residents along with absentee owners who visit the town during the milder months, utilizing the old homes as summer cabins.

WHAT'S TO SEE: There's an old—but still active—cemetery on the right a mile below the town. There are numerous dwelling houses, most in good condition, but no business houses. The views on the way up, especially after leaving North Bloomfield, are spectacular. (Bloomfield itself is a picturesque ghost town that, along with the nearby hydraulic diggins which afford hiking opportunities, is now a State Park. Each June they have a `Homecoming Days' and the town becomes alive once more. [Shades of Brigadooon!] You can easily spend a day there).

GETTING THERE: Take Highway 49 to Nevada City and turn left just past the town where a sign indicates Downieville. A few hundred yards further on turn right toward North Bloomfield. Stay on this road until you reach Graniteville, about 28 miles further on. Much of the road is gravel and while it can be negotiated by an ordinary sedan, about 20 miles of the way will be slow (15-25 MPH) driving. In inclement weather, don't attempt the trip as the town lies near 5000 feet and can get considerable snow.

FACILITIES: None in Graniteville—gasoline and provisions can be purchased in Nevada City.

TRAVEL TIME: 2.5 hours.

ALLEGHENY

Alleghany was first worked in 1853 when the Allegheny Company started a tunnel in the area. The town itself was laid out in 1856 with a post office being established the following year, 1857. The mines began a gradual decline in 1862 but just the same the district remained one of California's best producers.

The nearby Sixteen to One Mine, is still operating, possibly California's last active hardrock mine. Over the years, the Sixteen to One has produced $25,000,000.

The town weathered the 1920-1950s, losing population but not becoming completely dead. Today, the town holds 121 inhabitants, most preferring a somewhat solitary life in the mountains over the hurly-burly of the valley. Many commute to Grass Valley, Nevada City and even Sacramento to work.

WHAT'S TO SEE: The town is stretched along a narrow, tortured street, clinging precariously to the mountain side. There are many residential homes and one cafe and a museum—neither open the day I was there. A lower side street leads to the cemetery.

GETTING THERE: From Nevada City, take Highway 49 toward Downieville. About four miles past North San Juan, you will see the turnoff to Alleghany (Ridge Road) on your right. The town is about 14 miles further on over a paved road. But the town lies at 4419 feet—in winter, check road conditions first.

FACILITIES: A bar and a cafe may be open but, independent minded as the people are, you never can tell. The nearest gas is North San Juan, a historic near-ghost in its own right.

TRAVEL TIME: 2.25 hours.

A person could spend a lifetime of vacations just traipsing to and visiting all of California's Sierra ghost towns—in whatever state of being they are today. Some you'll find to have been restored to a genteel condition, largely filled with boutique and antique shops, some are decaying back into the ground and most are just gone. But even if you find only forest when finally arriving at a former ghost town, the journey is worth the trip.

END

Rough & Ready in 1857

ONE HUNDRED YEARS AGO

IN NEVADA COUNTY

JUNE-1895

by

Brad Prowse

It's been warm for June. Temperatures topped 100 in Grass Valley more than once and the dusty roads have been a problem. But the last few days of the month have seen a cooling period that—according to Foster's Weather Forecasts—might lead to rain.

The Derbec mine is scheduled for closing due to playing out of its ore. It is North Bloomfield's main employer with 35 men on the payroll.

Someone is stealing copies of the Union—the paper offers a $20.00 reward for their capture.

A load of groceries in Frank King's cart broke through the flooring. King dropped through the hole and was dragged as his horse dashed across the Board Street bridge. It was caught on Commercial St. and was not injured—but King was.

A colored Man, James Curtis, was arrested on the complaint of J. E. Parker, also a man of color, for stealing Parker's pistol. Curtis argued he took the pistol in self defense.

The Miners Union Picnic, held in Glenbrook Park, featured baseball, football, drilling contests, dancing and a horse race on which a large sum of money was staked.

Later, a Turk who had been selling trinkets at the picnic was beaten and robbed by two men.

The semi-annual examination of school teachers will take place at the county seat.

National Guard Companies C and H, of Nevada City and Grass Valley, respectively, are spending 10 days at a camp in Vallejo.

The Union notes happenings elsewhere:

Downieville's Chinatown was wiped out by a disastrous fire. Downieville itself was spared only after three charges of giant powder were used to demolish buildings.

And a great fire, raging for five hours, burned four blocks of San Francisco the other evening, doing 2 million dollars in damage and destroying the homes of 100 families. All the city's fire companies were needed to contain the conflagration.

In Lodi, Mrs. Cordway, the wife of a prominent farmer, horsewhipped a Salvation Army officer for slandering her.

In Healdsburg, a small band of Indians, seeking whisky, attacked a camp of Italian charcoal burners. One Indian was badly hurt in the melee.

Bodie is experiencing a rebirth with so many men flocking there that many must sit up all night in saloons due to lack of sleeping rooms.

Oklahoma Territory—Bill Doolin and his gang have been surrounded by lawmen in a cave in the Glass Mountains.

President Cleveland issued a proclamation warning all citizens not to give aid to the Cuban rebels.

Finally, at an Alabama ball, a man stepped on a woman's train. When the smoke had cleared, two men were dead and a score injured. One shudders to think what would have transpired if a man had danced twice with another's girl.

The Mining and Scientific Press says that mines in and around Nevada City and Grass Valley have been the mainstay of the California mining industry.

Local optician Louis Dorais has reading glasses—25 cents, 50 cents and one dollar.

Bicycle fever continues to rage and the local ladies practice on the machines in their cute bloomer costumes.

Delegates of the Grand Parlor of the Native Daughters had a chance to tour local mines. A few brave souls donned headgear and descended into the mines themselves.

Two young locals, angered over something, retired to Ragons Grove to engage in fisticuffs. Both are battered—one going to a doctor, the other applying a beefstake poultice to his eye.

All talk is about the upcoming 4th of July celebration in Grass Valley. 1500 Nevada Citians are expected to attend.

And the annual Cornish wrestling matches are scheduled in Grass Valley July 4th and 5th. $280 in prizes will be awarded.

A man had a touch of the snake yesterday and constable Dillon had him quartered at the city's bastille.

W. D. Harris, furniture dealer, has oak extension tables for $5.50 and 7 piece bedroom suites for $20.00.

The post of a Chinese laundry on Nevada City's main street was knocked out by a runaway horse and cart—no injuries.

The Union notes the worth of some foreign currencies against the dollar: (In cents) Franc, 19.3; Mark, 23.8; Mexican silver dollar, 47.9; Gold Yen, 99.7; Chinese Tael, 69; Silver Ruble, 35.3; Lira, 19.3; Rupee, 21;

Residents of Lost Hill are petitioning for a fire hydrant to be installed in their area.

It has been ordered that the Grass Valley road be sprinkled from the city limits to the plaza if citizens will raise the $10 per month needed for such work during the summer months.

The infant child of Mr. and Mrs. William Rule died yesterday afternoon.

E. M. Bachelde, A. P. Hodges and other drummers, well known in the city, have formed a Travelers Protective Association.

The Nevada City water works plans to replace 2200 feet of 11 inch pipe with 15 inch conduit, which should improve water pressure.

A valuable horse belonging to Henry Lane dropped dead suddenly after being ridden in from North San Juan.

Brace and Eddy's saloon was broken into—missing are 400 cigars, a bottle of whisky and 350 nickels from a slot machine.

There exists in Grass Valley a brutal coward, a most despicable wretch who deserves to be tied to a whipping post and severely lashed. James Fuller struck his wife in the face than choked her to stifle her screams. This is not the first time Mrs. Fuller, a faithful wife and true lady, has received harsh treatment at her husband's hands. There was strong talk last night of forming a party to properly chastise Fuller and teach him a lesson.

Michael Skeahan was killed in a Lowell Hill cave in.

Two tramps robbed a Chinese cabin near Red Dog Road of $1.50 and a pistol.

But tramps are giving Nevada City a wide berth. They seem to realize that the law officers will have none of them here.

A $30 reward has been offered to anyone finding the remains of Ah Fong who left the Baltic Mine for Graniteville January 20th and has not been heard from since.

A fine lot of young horses for work or driving—weighing from 1000 to 1400 pounds—can be seen at Sutton's Ranch opposite Glenbrook Park.

Don Swart, the photographer, received from the east an appliance for taking pictures after dark. Samples can be seen at Carr Brother's Drug store.

A very large drove of horses passed through Nevada City on their way to the high country.

Theatrical companies that have appeared in Nevada City in the last six months have failed to receive much patronage. Either people are tiring of these productions or their quality is suspect. A minstrel troupe, leg show or company with a brass band will usually draw a crowd but it's apparent that the show business is played out in the city for the time being.

The road between the two towns is pleasant to drive now that the county is spending $100 a month to have it sprinkled.

A horsedrawn hand organ has been doing the town the past few days. The confusion of sounds would give one chills and we believe the apparatus itself has the malaria.

The water in Deer Creek is running very low.

Luthargo Flaaigan, an orphan girl, died at the Convent this morning.

An assay of ore at the Bellafountain Mine in Willow Valley assays out at $338 per ton. The mine is proving to be a big profit maker.

A Grass Valley girl found a packet of her parents old love letters in the attic and proceeded to read them to her mother, substituting her name and her boyfriends for her mother and father's. Her mother forbade her to have anything to do with a young man who would write such sickening and disgusting stuff. When she handed the letters over to her mother to read, the house became so still one could hear the grass grow out in the yard.

U-BET and RED DOG

by

Brad Prowse

Red Dog and U-Bet...two old gold towns that have been reclaimed by the forestland a few miles east of Nevada City. Today only their cemeteries, badly vandalized, remain. Still, the dive there is short (if you live around Sacramento and environs) and the Sierra picturesque so it might be worth your time for a day trip to the foothills.

U-Bet (or You-Bet) was supposedly named after early-day saloonkeeper, Lazarus Beard who used the expression to excess. There are several versions of how Red Dog got its name, one involving a dog, another saying it was named after a Red Dog Hill in the lead district of Illinois.

Red Dog sprang up in 1852. An attempt to change the name to 'Brooklyn' was turned down—the Post Office said the name already existed in Alameda County—so the townspeople resigned to it and Red Dog it was. It saw several disastrous fires, one in 1859 and another in 1862. There were 200 souls living there in 1866 but soon after the mines in the area played out and much of the town—buildings and all—were moved up the road to U-Bet.

U-Bet was settled in 1857, about two miles further east on Red Dog Road. By 1864 there were 40 or 50 buildings in the town. It suffered the fate of so many early-day hamlets—bad fires in 1869 and again in 1873. U-Bet depended on hydraulic mining to a great degree and the Sawyer decision in 1880 shutting down hydraulic mining affected the town.

Just the same, unscrupulous mining men, such as Jerry Goodwin, continued to use the big water monitors, relying on spies to warn them when inspectors were coming or operating only at night.

There were four spectacular killings in U-Bet, occurring in 1903 and 1913—all involved Goodwin, who was killed himself in the second affray. Mining continued right up to World War II though the population was much reduced and most of the stores boarded up. In 1933 electricity was run in and the school was opened in 1935 after being closed for 16 years. But legal problems concerning one of the main mines there spelled disaster for U-Bet. The school closed for good in 1943 and the War finished the town off.

U-Bet/Red Dog can be reached through Colfax by traveling about 8 miles west on Highway 174 or from Grass Valley by driving east 5 miles. U-Bet road, a left from Grass Valley, a right from Colfax, is plainly marked.

Drive 5 miles on U-Bet road. At 4 miles in, U-Bet Road swings right suddenly, toward Rollins Lake. Ignore this change and continue on straight ahead. You are now on Red Dog Road.

At 5 miles in, look to your left and along the ridge you should see a chain-link fence. This is the cemetery. The pavement ends just passed this point and a rough but passable gravel road begins.

At 5.5 miles there's a terrific view of Chalk Bluff and the stark, barren hydraulic diggins themselves—bring your camera and wide-angle or panorama lens!

About a half mile further on, at the bottom of the grade, you may notice some fruit trees. This was once the town of U-Bet. Red Dog was at the 6.9 mile mark and at 7.1 there's a side road to your left. A few hundred yards down this road and bearing left, you will come to the Red Dog cemetery.

Colfax and Grass Valley have abundant facilities but food and gas is available along 174. There are several small 'eateries' that serve regular fare but specialize on apple cakes, pies and cookies, made from the area's own apples. Yum!

END

ONE HUNDRED YEAR AGO

IN NEVADA COUNTY

August, 96

by

Brad Prowse

August was warm but a real heat wave moved in on the 12th. It held until cooler weather prevailed around the 28th.

The great fire in downtown Grass Valley and the tragic death of Sheriff Douglass are still very much on everyone's lips.

The monetary loss of the fire is around $85,000 and in its aftermath, Grass Valley is passing an ordnance requiring new buildings in the business area to be constructed of brick or stone.

And City Marshal Dana B. Getchell has been chosen to fill the position of sheriff.

There was a social dance at Columbia Hill last night and a large number of people from the area attended.

Willford Haskins, employed at Weissenburger's novelty shop, was caught in a pulley powering a bandsaw and received some cuts and bruises.

A soda factory will open in Relief Hill soon.

The lead bar on the Downieville stage broke the other day, causing the driver to be thrown from the seat.

The sewer on Main Street is blocked and is causing a fearful stench.

The building occupied by the UNION was sold but the paper will remain—we have a three-year lease.

Pioneer John Hill, 77, who arrived hereabouts in 1852, breathed his last on San Juan Ridge.

There are over 5300 voters on the new county register.

The National Fruit Store now has an electric machine for making milk shakes.

R. G. McClutchan's milk wagon team took a run down Nevada Street the other day, scattering milk cans about.

And M. A. Lord's horse and buggy was scared by a locomotive whistle and ran into a six-horse team in the plaza—injures were slight.

Two saloon keepers have been arrested for violation of the 12 midnight closing ordnance.

Two men were badly injured at the Fortuna Mine when some dynamite caps they were working with exploded unexpectedly.

Richard Davies has been appointed teacher of the Blue Tent school.

A duel has been threatened between a Grass Valley man and a Nevada City man—all over the affections of a lady. Further hostilities are looked for.

A fine ledge of gold was struck at the Summit Mine.

Richard Noell has not sold out his blacksmith business. He leased it while he camps in the mountains, recuperating from a spate of poor health.

A number of ladies, along with their children, enjoyed a picnic at F. F. Cassidy's property near the Y.W.O.D. mine.

Haussman and Gilbert, tailors, attempted to defraud a insurance company, claiming fire losses on merchandise actually stored elsewhere. They were forced to accept $1.00 for their claim or face prosecution.

A handsome new brick building has been erected in Chinatown.

The Digger Indians are holding their annual campoodie just outside town.

Jeanette, the 4 month old daughter of Mr. and Mrs. Charles Marsh, died Sunday.

There was a big Democratic rally in town last tonight.

The rumor that Democratic candidate William Jennings Bryan was being driven around town caused crowds to follow a carriage until it was revealed it was just a couple out for a moonlight ride.

And every day Bryan and his stand on silver gains more strength in the area. Nevada City has always been a strong Republican town but their number will be reduced considerably this year.

District Attorney Riley was questioned about the houses of ill-fame on Bank Street that were burned out in the fire. He vowed they would not be allowed to reestablish themselves.

A large forest fire has ravaged the Penn Valley area. Several horses have been killed.

Reports state there is no truth in the rumor of a merging of Western Union Telegraph and Bell Telephone.

Green Ousley, the well-known colored man, was stricken with paralysis the other day. Dr. Jamieson feels he will recover.

King & Wolford, the lumber mill men, had a horse worth $400 die the other day.

Two men driving bicycles from Reno to Marysville passed through here.

A fire destroyed the narrow-gauge bridge near Colfax. A temporary structure will be thrown up as a proposed track realignment is in the works that will replace three bridges with one.

A Chinaman thought to be in excellent health died suddenly in Chinatown last night. A bookkeeper, the Celestial was a wealthy man.

A power plant is on the way to Downieville and they will soon have electric lights.

It is said the Holbrooke House will soon change hands.

NEWS ITEMS FROM ELSEWHERE:

A heat wave in the east has killed over 100 in New York City alone.

A British man-of-war has seized a Mexican island in the State of Coloma—purportedly for use as a coaling station.

A marshal's posse has overtaken a group of bank robbers in Skeleton Canyon, New Mexico Territory. One lawman has been killed and U.S. troops from Forts Bayard and Grant are being called in to help.

And infantry and cavalry have moved to protect Nogales which was attacked by Yaqui Indians. The Santa Rita Mountains are said to ablaze with Indian signal fires.

Rumors from London say Queen Victoria intends to retire in favor of the Prince of Wales.

A newspaper editor was asked if he'd ever seen a bald-headed woman. "No," he said. "Nor have I seen a woman waltzing around town in her shirtsleeves, a cigar between her teeth, nor a woman go fishing with a bottle on her hip, there to sit on the damp ground all day just to go home drunk, nor have I seen a woman rip off her coat and say she could lick any man in the house. God bless her! She's not built that way!"

END

With a thirty foot diameter, this was the largest Pelton wheel ever made. It can still be seen at the North Star Mine Museum in Grass Valley.

This close-up of a Pelton wheel bucket plainly shows the divider that allows the water stream to 'split'

WHEEL OF FORTUNE

by

Brad Prowse

One day, over a hundred years ago, Lester Pelton watched as water from a garden hose splashed off a cow's nose—and it gave him an idea. And today that idea helps to generate the electricty that lights up your home. Here's how it's supposed to have happened:

Lester Allen Pelton was tired that day, tired and bored. He'd been working in his little shop, tinkering around with a new kind of water wheel, trying to find a way to improve it. Finally, disgusted at his lack of progress, he decided to take a break. He left the little shed behind his landlady's house and walked next door to his neighbor's yard where the man was about to chase a pesky cow back into its pasture.

The man directed a stream of water at the cow's face with a garden hose. As the water hit the sharp angle of the animal's nose it sprayed away in two seperate streams instead of splashing more-or-less randomly back as it would have off a flat surface. Pelton watched for a moment and then turned and went back to his shop, bored no more. He now had the answer to his problem, an answer that would make him wealthy and also, one day, help bring electricty to people all over the world.

Lester Pelton was born in Ohio in 1829. At 20 he heeded the siren song of the California Gold Rush and showed up around the bustling mining town of Camptonville, about 90 miles north-east of Sacramento, a burgeoning river town not yet the state capitol. He worked at a number of jobs—miner, millwright, carpenter—and displayed an enquiring and inventive nature.

The California gold fields quickly moved away from panning and placer mining. By the 1860's much of the gold gathering had gone underground as hard-rock miners scratched away at the rich ore-bearing quartz. If there was still plenty of gold to be coaxed out of the ground, there was a scarcity of power to do it with—power to run the pumps, the drills, the hoisting machinery. Gas and electric motors were still too primitive and steam engines were bulky to move and costly to run. But water was everywhere in the Sierras and ditches and wooden flumework could deliver water almost anywhere, as long as it was downhill. So, waterwheels began to be used for a power source.

At first over and under-shot wheels were employed, familiar to the influx of miners since they'd been used in the east since Colonial times. This is the type of wheel John Sutter had at Coloma, California when James Marshall discovered those few flakes of yellow that started a worldwide stampede and, incidently, impoverished his boss, Sutter. But by the 1860's and 70's the impulse wheel, running in an upright position with a series of `buckets' or vanes attached to the rim of the wheel had come into vogue. It was turned by the force of a stream of water directed against the buckets. Power was taken off the turning shaft with belts or gears. These wheels were simple to make but had one glaring fault; they weren't very efficient. They generated more power than the old over-undershot wheels, but were still inadequate for the needs of the ever expanding underground mines.

Pelton, a natural handyman, was working in the middle of what had become an area of hydralic mining activity. In this method of mining gold, huge water cannons, called monitors, were used to wash down entire hillsides. They threw gigantic streams of water against them, piped in from distant ponds through the ditch systems.

Monitors were incredibly powerful (and ecologically disasterous—they would be outlawed in the 1880's because of the damage they did). Pelton took an interest when he saw how the same water that tore down mountains could also be harnessed to turn a wheel.

The big problem with the impulse wheels was the way they utilized the water delivered to them. Water was sent down from lakes or holding ponds, using a systems of ditches, to finally be directed through long lengths of pipes and then out a small hose opening and played into the buckets on the wheel. This is what turned the wheel...and saw to it that it wouldn't turn very fast. Water splashing back from one bucket would hit the underside of the next bucket in line, limiting the speed of the wheel. Pelton, along with a number of other inventors of that time, started working on a way to eliminate this `backsplash' and increase the speed, and hence, efficency, of the wheels.

Pelton constructed his first impulse wheel in a shed in his landlady's back yard. It was a small one made of wood. He convinced his landlady, a Mrs. Groves, to let him hook it up to her treadle sewing machine. Sewing machines were major household appliances in those days, not inexpensive, and it was probably with some trepidation that Mrs. Groves looked on while Pelton played a garden hose against the buckets of his little wheel...which worked! The sewing machine ran.

But the splashback problem was still there and Pelton resolved to find a way to get around it...and then came the rambling ruminate. When Pelton saw the stream of water from the hose divide, going off at angles, away from what could be a line of buckets on a wheel, he knew he had the answer. And that answer, beautiful in its simplicity, was to cast a dividing wall down the center of each bucket, running vertically in the same plane the wheel traveled. This caused the incoming stream of water to split in two, both streams flying off to the sides and away from the bucket above.

It took a while to perfect, but Pelton's final design used a spoon shaped bucket with a sharp ridge in the middle of the `spoon' that deflected the water away from the next bucket in line. Pelton finally had a satisfactory version running by 1878 and 2 years later, won his patent.

Now admittedly, the cow story is just one of a couple that has risen to explain how Pelton came up with the idea of splitting the water. Another was that he noticed a turning wheel increase in speed when the key holding it on the shaft became loose, allowing water to hit the side of the bucket, partly diverting the splashing water to one side. But in a cow's nose or a pig's eye, he found a way to improve the old impulse wheels and it was to make Pelton's fortune.

Initially, Pelton had his wheels made at the Nevada City Foundry in Nevada City, California, about 60 miles from Sacramento, by now the state capitol. At first the wheels were made of wood with cast iron buckets. This proved to be unsatisfactory. The wood shrank from the constant wetting and drying of the water which caused the buckets to loosen. Finally, a cast iron wheel with iron buckets proved to be the answer. But orders came in so fast that Pelton had to relocate to San Francisco where he met A.P. Brayton, a machine shop operator, and they founded the Pelton Water Wheel Company in 1888.

Pelton's wheels quickly went into service around the world. Some were used to power the first electric light systems in many American cities and others replaced the steam engines that the mines had been using. Pelton wheels were installed at the 1,680 foot level of the Chollarshaft Mine in Virginia City, Nevada to drain the Sutro tunnel. A pelton wheel in Switzerland used a head (distance water dropped from source to wheel) of 5,740 feet and other wheels developed up to 70,000 horsepower. Worldwide, Pelton wheels today are the machines used for generating electricty in hydro-electric dams.

Pelton died in 1908, leaving no family. In his lifetime, he saw to the building of wheels as small as 4 inches in diameter, used for running sewing machines, dental equipment, ect., to wheels as large as 20 feet across.

With the coming of electricty and the electric motor, and later the closing of most of the mines, many of the older Pelton wheels, designed for the hardrock mines of California, were replaced or abandoned. But one Pelton wheel, at thirty feet across, the largest ever built, still stands near the old North Star Mine in Grass Valley California, a town about three miles south of Nevada City. Now part of a mining exhibit and museum, the giant wheel was used to provide compressed air to the underground drills, hoists and pumps in the North Star. Fed by a 20 inch diameter water pipe, it turned at 65 RPM and developed 1000 horsepower.

The giant wheel was shut down in 1933. Only once was an attempt made to restart it when a temporary power shortage loomed. But as the great wheel started to turn, water, rushing through ancient casings, began to strain at the pipe seams. Finally the order to shut down the water was given and the mighty wheel was stilled, forever.

It is said that when Edison died, the thought occurred to someone that all the lights in America should be turned off for one minute, as a final tribute. But the idea was abandoned when it was pointed out the world was now too dependent on Edison's inventions to be without them, even for a minute. Lester Pelton was no such lofty a genius as Edison was, but if it were not for Pelton's wonderous wheel, Edison, the Wizard of Menlo Park, would have had a harder time generating the electricty that coursed through his light bulbs.

END

ONE HUNDRED YEARS AGO

IN NEVADA COUNTY

NOVENMBER, 1896

by

Brad Prowse

Almost an inch of rain fell on the first. Then heavy rains persisted—on and off—throughout the month with the year to date total at November's end being almost 15 inches.

The UNION has gone to great expense to receive election returns on Tuesday, the 3rd. Nevada City will be provided with bulletins.

If you are putting your wheel away for the winter, be sure to cover the frame thoroughly in Vaseline and wrap the rest in old rags and hang it up in a dry place. In the spring, it will be as good as new.

And in the east, an inventor has designed a chainless bicycle that uses beveled gears to drive the rear wheel.

McKinley has been elected president, though Nevada County went for Bryan. However, Smartsville, for the first time, voted Republican—watch out for the millennium!

A William Coabus signed a contract betting his wife in the late election. If Bryan had won, she was to have gone to another. Such a man does not deserve a good wife and no court in the land would uphold such a heinous contract.

An accident on board the Battleship `Texas' has caused it to ship water. It lies at a Brooklyn dock, submerged five feet above its waterline.

In New York, the Knights of Labor passed a resolution today calling for a graduated income tax.

A horrible tale from Alaska where a man named Wells apparently died and was buried. Six months later, his wife in New Jersey asked that the body be sent to her. The body was exhumed and when the casket was opened, Wells' body was found on its side. In his hand was his partial plate and there was evidence he tried to claw his way out of the coffin.

Rolfe Buffington fractured his left ankle playing football in the schoolyard.

D. T. Darnoven of Forest Springs will push four of Clinch & Company's employees around town in a wheelbarrow to pay off an election bet. A band may be hired and spectators are invited to join in.

The Curly Bears will hold a dance Wednesday.

A woodpile at the rear of Jenny Taylor's bagnio caught fire. It was quickly extinguished.

And several buildings at the Good Hope Mine at Cabbage Patch were burned to the ground—a loss of $1200.

Last month's bullion output at the Champion Mine was very large.

The Bell Brothers have shut down their Snow Tent and Granetville sawmills for the season.

Considerable interest is being manifested locally in the coming Sharkey-Fitzsimmons fight in San Francisco.

Scores of new building permits were let this summer and even as the weather worsens, many new dwellings are under construction.

Hugh McCauley's four-year old daughter died yesterday at Cherokee.

Charles Wolfe was arrested for battery against two women of the half-world, Mabel Foster and May Lenard. Wolfe, basking in the women's smiles, decided that one had stolen a dollar from him and he attempted to take revenge.

James Cary was kicked by his horse and had his collarbone broken.

Small boys breaking windows have Marshall Levee on the prowl.

Officers Shoemaker and Ryan broke up row between John Seville and Albert Harris. Harris pulled a dagger on Seville and was at a loss to explain why he carried such a weapon.

Pearce, the champion Cornish wrestler of the world and well known around here, died in Redding.

It was payday at several mines and the town was lively last night.

Nevada City has nearly 100 telephones.

William McAdams, the saloon keeper, was found guilty of adultery.

Truckee is getting ready for its Ice Carnival.

And J. Cuneo has been arrested in Truckee for selling liquor to Indians. Frank Sour and John Patterson were being held as witnesses.

There was a serious row among the Monoglians in Chinatown last night when Jim How, a disgruntled player, made off with some winnings that weren't his.

There have been reports from reliable citizens of a large airship being spotted overhead at night in the Sacramento Valley. An inventor, William Warren, from Haywards, claims he has such a ship, that it flys at one hundred feet, that it carries one man and that it is powered by a gasoline engine.

Sheriff Getchell's home will soon be lighted by electricity.

The National Hotel served over 250 people Thanksgiving evening.

A contract to build a new steel bridge across Wolf Creek near Perrins's was awarded to Cotton Brothers for $1690.

Mrs. Music is having a new house built on Adams Street.

Students brought a complaint against high-school teacher J. W. Reese to the Board of Education the other night. They claimed he was not polite to them and often used unbecoming expressions such as alluding to a historical female figure as 'large busted.'

A shopkeeper hired a young lad to work for him but the boy's clothes were in such a sorry state that the kindly shopkeeper outfitted him in new clothes with the agreement that the boy would pay for them out of future wages.

On the following Monday, the boy was nowhere to be seen. When the shopkeeper inquired of the lad's mother as to his whereabouts, she said, "He has such fine clothes, now, that he's out trying to get a better job."

ONE HUNDRED YEARS AGO

December, 1896

In Nevada County

by

Brad Prowse

Rain at the first of December and heavy rains mid-month, then clear until the end when snow fell.

Israel Hosken paid $20 for violating the midnight closing ordinance.

Tonight, the Union will be receiving reports on the Sharkey-Fitzsimmons fight in San Francisco.

Some beautiful ore specimens were taken from the Pennsylvania Mine yesterday.

And the Morningstar Mine at Iowa Hill paid a $3.00 per share dividend.

Sharkey was knocked out by Fitzsimmons in the eighth round but referee Wyatt Earp gave the decision to Sharkey on a foul no one else was able to see. Earp, a notorious border gun fighter, was fined $50 for wearing a large pistol into the ring.

Officer Loher arrested a hobo picking pockets among the throng listening to the Union reports.

There'll be a turkey shoot at the Adams Ranch Saturday.

And the class of '96 will meet tonight at the Lincoln schoolhouse.

In Philadelphia, the cruiser, Brooklyn, was added to the Navy's arsenal.

The Reno baseball club has accepted the Popular's challenge. A match game will be played at Watt Park on the 13th for $100 a side.

David R. Steel, of Auburn Road, died. He was a Mexican War veteran.

People in North Bloomfield claimed they saw an airship. So did those in Granitville—but theirs turned out to be a hot air balloon with a candle in it sent up by some wag.

The W.A.P.A. will give a `Darky cake walk' and basket social in their hall on the 17th.

President Cleveland said it is not yet time to recognize Cuba, despite congressional pressure to do so. Spain says recognition of Cuba will be an act of war.

And an Ohio newspaper is encouraging army veterans to join an armed movement to free Cuba.

J. W. Reese, the teacher complained about last month by students, will be discharged at the end of the school term. Reese says he will sue.

A competing stageline now runs between Grass Valley and Marysville.

The Masonic building on the corner of Pine and Commercial is receiving a new roof.

East Lynne was produced by the Bates-Ward Company at the theater last night.

Sheriff Getchell, grading some land on his property, found a five dollar goldpiece from the 1850s and a dime dated 1823.

Remember: Donation Day on the 18th—have your stick and potato ready. Nevada City will have their first Donation Day this year.

Lillioukalani, ex-queen of Hawaii, is visiting San Francisco.

For the second time, boys have broken the incandescent light in front of Argall's shop. If they don't make amends today, warrants will be issued for their arrest.

Bennett Moyle received a fractured jaw at the Randolph Mine when hit by a hoist bucket.

Nevada City merchants will stay open until 9 PM during the Holidays.

James Will's saloon on Pine Street was ransacked—no doubt done by the same old gang.

And Ott's assay office was also burglarized. But Mr. Ott is too cautious to leave bullion around.

The athletic club put on an exhibition. John Granholm gave a fine demonstration of contortion work.

Neavis Garcia, who sold pasties and tamales on the streets, has died at Basso's boardinghouse.

It is asserted that a Grass Valley lady at a dance tapped her husband gently on the shoulder with her fan and said, "Love, it's growing late. We had better go home."

Once there, the woman brandished a rolling pin and said, "You infamous old snaggle-toothed scoundrel, you, if you ever look at the mean, hateful, calico-faced, mackerel-eyed old thing your eyes were riveted on tonight, I'll burst your coconut wide open for you."

J. H. Annabel and William Pascoe have been appointed guardians of the minor children of the Late Sheriff Pascoe.

We hear that Browns Valley will soon have a commercial bank. The sporting element there already have a faro bank…

The bad weather may delay the erection of an Ice Carnival in Truckee.

There was a chimney fire in the Catholic parsonage—$100 damage done.

And the Union received news of a large fire in Jamestown. Also, the stage between Auburn and Georgetown was held up and the Wells-Fargo box taken.

Train robberies, too, still are in vogue; one reported from Texas and another in Missouri.

Beware—chicken thieves have struck several times of late.

A demented man roaming about Deadmans Flat has the residence worried.

A rumor from Sacramento says the legislature is about to levy a $300 per year tax on all saloons.

Two Sacramento Girls, one not yet 16, were inveigled by a miscreant, presently in Sheriff Getchell's Hotel, to come to Grass Valley and work in a bagnio. One girl was returned to Sacramento by way of a warrant against her for the $80 she stole of her grandmother's money to make the trip. The other yet serves in the sporting house, left to contemplate her fate in this world.

A 16 year-old Chinese slave girl, Wan Kim, bought from her parents in China to become a bride in San Francisco, was instead sold for $1750 to a wealthy merchant. She managed to escape and is in the hands of the Children's Society.

The streets present an animated appearance as Christmas Day approaches. Goynes Band and carolers were out, attracting crowds. Most churches are holding services Christmas Eve.

Teamsters would appreciate a watering trough in the plaza.

Dr. C. W. Jones, standing on his porch, fired five shots at Thomas Horan, wounding him in the wrist. Horan, who owns a bus used to carry miners to work, and Mrs. Jones, confessed to seeing each other clandestinely. The Doctor was released on a $1000 bond.

There have been at least seven horse-and-team runaways this month. Fortunately, damage and injures have been slight but such occurrences pose a constant threat to the populace.

In New York, a young artist's model was arrested for indecent exposure because she posed in the nude. Her father brought the charges.

A fine, self-cocking revolver has been found by B. Bullard. The owner can have the weapon by proving it's his and paying for this ad.

Jack Pollock's cabin, near U-Bet Station, was blown up. He was drying giant powder on his stove. Pollock probably will not live.

North San Juan was practically deserted Christmas night thanks to a Dance at Columbia Hill.

The prisoners at the county jail enjoyed a fine, turkey dinner from the New York Hotel, along with plenty of delicacies.

"Did you know your confounded dog barks all night long?" one neighbor yelled at another.

"Yes, I suppose he does," the man said. "But don't worry about him. He makes up for it by sleeping all day."

An old hoist frame at the Lava Cap mine still reaches skyward

SLEEPING GIANT

The Lava Cap Gold Mine

by

Brad Prowse

By a twist of fate, the three largest producing gold mines in California history were situated within a few miles of each other in the Sierra Nevada foothills. In descending order of output they were the Empire Mine, the Idaho-Maryland Mine and the Lava Cap Mine. All are located in Nevada County, the Empire and the Idaho-Maryland laying close to downtown Grass Valley, the Lava Cap settled in an area almost as pristine as when it was operating, fifty years ago.

Today, the Empire is a flooded hulk, a state park where people can roam about, wondering at its massive concrete pinnings, rusting machinery and a towering headframe, still standing magnificent sentry over a shaft.

The Idaho-Maryland Mine, a little over a mile away from the Empire, has become almost obliterated by a profusion of small businesses and manufacturers that have camouflaged the old mine property with portables and tin-roofed shops of one kind and another.

Six miles away from the Idaho-Maryland is the Lava Cap Mine. The Lava Cap sits just south of Banner Mountain, below its brooding ridge, many of its buildings intact, its headframe still proudly punching seventy-five feet into the sky. With around $40,000,000 in gold reserves banked in its granite vaults, it's one of the most complete and ready to go of California's former great mines if again the order to commence mining is given.

The area from Auburn, California south to Yosemite was considered the Mother Lode of the great Gold Rush of `49. From Auburn north to around Downieville became known as the Northern Mines. Though gold was discovered in the Northern Mines area only a few years later, it's often overlooked by the aura various colorful books and stories by the likes of Twain, Bret Harte, et al, have given us of rough miners wresting gold in the early camps of the Mother Lode. In truth, the Northern Mines were richer and operated for a longer time than did those in the Mother Lode.

The last of the mines, mostly in and around Grass Valley, finally shut down in 1956, stilled by a combination of low gold prices and labor demands by the unions. But if most mines have settled back into the dirt, become surrounded by suburbs, turned into industrial parks or been preserved as showcases, The Banner Lava Cap Mine has neither succumbed to the elements nor become hemmed in by developments.

The area that today is known as the Lava Cap Mine actually started out as two individual mines—the Banner and the Central. The Banner was discovered first, in 1860. The area is covered with a cap of lava that is as deep as 100 feet but that had become exposed at both ends. One story has it that Hawaiian miners, used to seeing such formations in their native land, first noted the outcropping. The next year the Central was discovered, about 4,500 feet south of the Banner.

A group of men, including three named Jeffery, Rolfe and Withington, formed the Douglas Company to explore the claim. They sank a 75 foot shaft but soon abandoned the mine. In the next few years the Banner would be taken over and abandoned by several companies until, in 1865, Messrs. Kidd, Styles, Rich, Tisdale and Tilton began work in earnest. Then Kidd sold out and the others merged with three more men, Head, Morrow and Land, calling themselves the Banner Company.

A mill with ten stamps was erected in 1867. From May, 1866 to June, 1871, $550,486 was taken from the Banner with $48,000 in dividends paid out. Still, the company was dissolved and the mine lay idle. Then a J. E. Brown obtained a patent of 1,500 feet adjoining the old mine and new stock was issued with capitol of $2,000,000 raised in 1879. By 1880, the Banner mine complex had yielded about $775,000.

The mines were located in a fault area where molten, gold bearing quartz moved into a rift caused eons ago when the earth shifted. In the Banner and Central mines this fault ran from 2 to 32 feet in width. But unlike some mines, most of the gold and silver was in very fine flakes, not the nuggets and clusters found in other local mines.

Recovery with the methods of the day were quite inefficient, Using the primitive stamp mills and mercury amalgamation plates and tables, the best they could expect was about 40% and often as low as 27%—this with gold at around $18-an ounce.

The Banner milled about 20,000 tons of ore at $20-$30 a ton but eventually it pinched out around 1906 at the 800 foot level and the mine closed. The Central was also operated spasmodically over the years. It proved to be a good producer of silver—about 4 parts of silver for 1 of gold—but had the same problem with recovery. It closed down around 1917. Between the two mines, about $1,000,000 to $2,000,000 in gold was produced by the end of the 1870s, but after that, production faltered.

The two mines had been run as separate entities up to the time they closed down in the early years of the 20th century.

There was an attempt to reorganize the mines in 1922 under the name Banner Consolidated Mines, Co. It's probably at this time the three mines—the Central, Banner and North Banner—were placed under one management but no real work was done until the early 1930s when another reorganization was accomplished by the Lava Cap Gold Mining Corporation, a Canadian outfit. They floated 1,600,000 shares of stock, raising $2,500,000.

This was to be a earnest attempt to wrest a profit out of the old holes. The workings in the Central were dewatered—there was need to only run the pumps every other day—and the upper portions of the shaft were enlarged and retimbered. In the Banner, the Belshaw shaft—an inclined shaft—was pumped to the 800 foot level and the drift continued to 2,500 feet.

A new, state-of-the-art gold refining system was installed. This consisted of two jaw crushers and a cone crusher. Once the ore was reduced to small pieces of rock, it was weighed and then sent to the ball and rod mill, weighed again—to make sure none had been highgraded—and went on to further processing. By this time, the ore was almost the consistency of flour.

The Kraut Flotation Machine, a German device, was used to 'float' the gold in a slurry that allowed it to be skimmed. The resultant product then when to another building were it was further processed in huge cyanide vats. The resultant concentrate, called the pregnant solution, was trucked to Shelby Smelters in the Bay Area. There, the solution was 'burned' to remove all the contaminants. What was left was the gold and silver.

The new recovery rate was in the order of 94% to 95%. In the years the mine was actually operating—1934-1943—it produced around $12,000,000 in gold and silver, this when gold was at $35 an ounce and silver at 60-80 cents an ounce. The Lava Cap mines would turn out to be the third largest producers of gold in California and the largest gold mine that also produced silver—primarily out of the Central, which had a strong silver vein. The mines produced between a third to a half ounce of gold per ton.

But this level of production would take awhile to reach. New mine buildings had to be built, and a 300 ton mill installed. In 1937 the wood headframe was replaced by an iron frame, made by the Schrader Iron Works in San Francisco. This frame was pre-drilled at the factory so accurately that it took only one day to replace the old headframe. The majority of this work was done at the Central Mine site. The mine even had its own wood mill to make lumber.

In the early 1930s, the mine operated at a loss. A report filed in 1935 by a C. W. Van Law of Toronto, probably sent by the headquarters in Ontario, praised the Lava Cap operations generally but was critical of Otto Schiffner, the general manager of the mines. He complained that Schiffner was wasting time and effort in workings that didn't look promising. Apparently Schiffner wanted to extend the mines deeper, into territory that Van Law didn't feel was productive. He questioned Schiffner's going after "worthless" ore.

But Schiffner was vindicated. In 1937, another report by two other men—L. K. Fletcher and J. H. Rattray, of Ontario, Canada—stated that the mine had become productive earlier that year. By April of 1937, the books showed a profit of $70,639. By year's end, there was a profit of $510,000 and a 20 cents per share dividend had been declared.

The mines were processing 390 tons of ore a day. In 1935, 5,000 tons of ore per month was being milled, 1800 from the Banner, 3,200 from the Central. The Banner received its electric power from the Central and both operated electric ore trams. At its peak, 310 miners, bussed in from Grass Valley, would be employed. An unusually large percentage of them were Italian.

The mine ran three shifts and the men were paid from portal-to-portal—when entering and exiting the mine. A miner or timberman made $5.84 a day, switchmen and muckers, $5.36 a day and hoistmen $6.72 a day, not bad pay for a country in depression but it was hard, dirty dangerous work.

One of the main goals was the joining of the two mines, the Banner and the Central. It was believed—and proved true—that the two were working on opposite ends of the same vein. It would be advantageous to join the two with a common shaft following this vein. This would reduce trucking costs—having to send ore by road to the Central from the Banner—and allow the Central to utilize the natural ventilation of the mine interior that the Banner enjoyed. The tunnel was finally competed at the 650 foot level. It was 8,000 feet long. There were over 32 miles of works between the two mines and the Central went to 32 levels.

There is a story of a ghost—Charlie—that the miners felt was their friend. Once when ore deposits seemed to be running low and their Holiday bonus of a turkey—along with the continuation of their jobs—looked slim, the foreman awoke one night and felt a compulsion to enter the mine. There a ghostly figure beckoned him to a certain spot that seemed to glow.

The foreman returned to bed but woke again later and went to the mine owner and both went to the spot indicated by 'Charlie.' There they found a new vein—and everyone got their turkey.

The Lava Cap mines were still prospering when the order came to shut down. World War II had begun and gold mining wasn't considered essential to the war effort. The men in the mines could be better used in the shipyards—or the front lines. In 1943, with over $40,000,000 in reserves, (today's prices) the Lava Cap mines closed down.

Now the area did experience a depression of sorts. From a high of 20,000 people in Nevada County, the population dropped to around 14,000. It wasn't to reach the former number again until the late 1970s.

When the war ended, some of the mines opened again—but not the Lava Cap. The low price of gold—$35 an ounce—coupled with higher labor rates, kept some mines from opening. In 1956 a general strike by the miners caused even the operating mines to throw in the towel. The mines were closed for good. Or where they…?

In 1952 the New Goldvue Mines, Ltd., of Toronto, Canada bought the Lava Cap. Apparently they did little with it though and in 1978 a Tracy Hudgins and Ruth Flax leased the properties. Hudgins was a chemist and had worked for the famous Homestake mine in Canada.

Then, owners of homes that had moved near the perimeter of the mine property over the years became worried about noise, traffic and the affect on local wells. They gathered 800 signatures, trying to block the dewatering of the Central. The county required Hudgins to devise a system to monitor local wells. In the face of the opposition, the mine stayed closed.

Somewhere between these last two owners, much mining equipment was sold off, principally the machine shop, supplies and large parts of the mining plant. Left was the headframe, compressors, dewatering equipment and most of the major buildings.

One last attempt to open the mine was made in 1984 by the Franco-Nevada Corporation. They had about all their paperwork done and permits in hand when neighboring homeowners got an injunction and stopped the reopening of the mine.

The present owner of the mine is Steve Elder, 54. Born in Huntington Beach and raised around China Lake, his background is construction and development, not mining. He has the thick arms and barrel chest of a man who knows physical labor.

"I knew I wanted to own this place the minute I saw it,"

Elder said, as he gave me a tour of the mine buildings. "Not to work the mine—to live. So, in 1988, I bought it. Own 2500 acres of mineral rights and 110 acres of surface land."

"The mine facilities have held up pretty well," Elder said as we walked into a large room that held rows of low tables. Suspended from the ceiling and spaced around were sets of 'spokes,' some holding small tin cans. Each could be raised by its own cable.

"This was the change room. The miners hung their street clothes on the spokes, put their valuables in the cans, and pulled the whole thing to the ceiling with the cable. Gave them a measure of security."

"Most of the buildings are still in pretty good shape," Elder said. "But some have caved in, like that one there," Elders said, pointing to a shambles of tin, wood framing and several large, iron wheels. "Those were idler wheels that supported the cable going from the winch to the headframe."

Elder took me through an area that had been the office. Scattered about on a shelf were a bunch of 60 year-old canceled paychecks, the name of the miners still visible. In the old safe, just off the cyanide room, was a file cabinet full of employee records, listing name, date of employment, position and so forth.

"The mine itself is flooded—about thirty miles of works," Elder said. "It'd take six months to pump it all out. That's what the nearby homeowners worried about most. The mine itself wouldn't involve that much traffic or noise. It was the wells."

People in Nevada County depended on fractures in the ground rock to supply water to their wells, most at the two-three hundred foot level. Hydraulic studies say that dewatering a mine with workings so much lower than the local wells probably would have no affect on them. But the only way to find out is to pump out the mine...

In the winter of 1996-7 a dam in a holding pond just below the mine burst, allowing water containing arsenic to flow into Little Clipper Creek and on down to Lost Lake, about two miles away. At the time, it caused a fair amount of consternation in the neighborhood. I asked Elder about the arsenic—and the cyanide that was used to process the ore.

"Cyanide is no problem," Elder said. "Stuff dissipates into the air and is gone without doing any harm. Arsenic is something else."

"Arsenic is found in the ore," Elder said. "It gets processed out and left in the tailings. In the old days, the mine water leached through the tailings and into the pond. Then the water spilled out over the pond dam—that's the way they handled it. I have old movies that show them running water out of the pond in the 1930s or 40s and it's the same, milky color we got when the dam broke two winters ago."

"Lost Lake was built by the mine! It was designed to be another catch basin for the mine water. Only, people have moved in since then and turned the place into a residential area. As far as we can tell, no one around here has ever gotten sick over the arsenic, the recent spill or when the mine was open."

"Anyway, after the spill, the EPA people came in and filled in the pond—with more tailings! Go figure."

"I know there's some concern I'll open the mine again," Elder said. "Won't happen. I did make up some ore samples along with a history of the mine, put them in glass bottles and tried to sell them. Wanted to raise enough to repair some of the buildings, but it didn't work out."

"This is my home," Elder said. "I live in one of the old mine buildings and I'm building a new home over there, just above the headframe. I sold off the old Banner mine land—did keep the mineral rights, though. And I developed a few lots on the edge of the property, up near the Nevada County Airpark. But I'm no miner."

Elder was quiet for a few moments. Perhaps he was thinking about gold's 5,000 year intimacy with humans and how, over the eons, man has always returned to search for the precious metal when forces social or financial become precarious enough.

"I will say this," Elder finally offers. "If gold gets back up to $400 an ounce, I would not be surprised to see a lot of old mines reopen around here."

So the Lava Cap Mine continues to sit, like a great, gray goose, her tin skirts pulled down snugly around her golden eggs, pondering her fate and wondering if men again will come to scratch for her treasure—or, if history is any teacher, when.

END

ONE HUNDRED YEARS AGO
IN NEVADA COUNTY

MAY, 1897

by

Brad Prowse

The last of a series of social dances given by the hydraulic Parlor of Native Sons and the Laurel Parlor of Native Daughters was held at the Odd Fellows Hall last night. Goyne's Band provided the music.

Willie George, an Indian, lies cold in death at the undertaker's parlor. He was stabbed near the race track on the Nevada Road by a half-breed known as Frank Tom. Tom has been arrested.

A round trip on the Narrow Gauge between Nevada City and Grass Valley is now 40 cents, down a dime.

Some thief cleaned up the sluices of T. L. Canfield's claim at Selby Flat Friday night.

A couple of Chinamen engaged in a fight in a store in the Mongolian center last night. It was said to have been a lively scrap. The principal weapon, a bowl, was wielded by a cook.

Work on the ballground in Watt Park is about completed.

John Bianchi, an Italian barber arrested in Nevada City for adultery, has received 6 months in the county jail.

An incandescent lamp in the H.C. Mills home on Main street burned out of its socket and landed on a bed, starting a fire. It was quickly contained.

In Houston, a mob of Negroes lynched six of their own people for the murder of a colored family.

Dr. C.W. Jones was called to Rough & Ready last evening. He dressed a bullet wound in the hand of a fourteen-year old boy who had been playing with a pistol.

Five or six more telephones will be installed around town in the next few days.

Fighting between the Turks and Greeks has become fierce with many reports of Turkish soldiers mutilating Greek prisoners. Greek women and children have leapt to their deaths to escape dishonor.

The watering trough placed in the Plaza by the city fathers is a desirable improvement.

For the next few weeks, the Nevada County Electric Company will divert the South Yuba river to allow the mining of four miles of bedrock.

In a shooting scrape at Dobbins Ranch, a man named Page tried to use a Winchester on superintendent Daily of the Good Title Mine. The rifle misfired—Daily's pistol didn't. Page, a former employee, is in the hospital and Daily is in jail.

Ah Lung, a wealthy merchant who had a store on Commercial Street has been robbed while traveling about China. Lung left this area two years ago. He is married to a highly educated Chinese maiden from North San Juan.

The sewer election will not take place next Monday as the legality of the proceedings are in question.

A few days ago a man claiming to have lost both hands in a mining accident showed up at the Champion Mine. He touched many hearts and gathered $50. He then proceeded to the nearest saloon where he drank away all his alms. He presently resides in the city jail.

Pugilists Eddy Shannon and Lee Agnew fought a terrific battle in Michigan that referees tried to break up three times without success. Both men, bruised and bloody, finally collapsed in the 46th round.

W.B. Bourn, principal owner of the Empire Mine, will build a $30,000 summer residence on Ophir Hill. The exterior walls will be roughhewn granite two feet thick while the interior will be done entirely in natural wood.

Charles Poole, an old prospector who lived on Deer Creek, was found dead of natural causes near his cabin yesterday.

The North Star Mining Company commenced work on a new shaft on Massachusetts Hill.

Alleen Olivia, the four-year old daughter of Mr. and Mrs. Thomas Keleher, died of bronchitis.

W.H. Turner, the blind man, purchased the variety business of Philip Trezise.

The Idaho National Guard Armory was broken into and 75 arms taken.

The Indians will have a big cry at their campoodie tonight over the death of Willie George.

Senator McMullin of Arkansas attempted to kill the editor of the Arkansas Gazette, Mr. Smithee, who was able to deflect the Senator's pistol barrel. McMullin was released on bail but more trouble is likely.

Manual Marks, twelve, has been arrested at the instigation of his father who claims the boy is wild and needs to be in reform school. Upon examination, many bruises and injuries inflicted by the father were found on the boy. The case deserves to be investigated further before action is taken.

Eight years ago, a Piute Indian murdered some white men in Southern Nevada. The whites in the area said Aheote, his brother, must bring them his head, which he did. Brooding about it ever since, Aheote went on the warpath not long ago and killed four whites. Local miners claimed if Aheote's head wasn't brought in, they would kill every Piute they could. A standoff between Indians and whites threatened but in the end, Aheote's body was brought in by the Piutes. But fifty miles north at White Hill, 15 armed Piutes are threatening to kill whites.

A new organ for the Methodist Church is expected from Chicago any day now.

Tomorrow, Deputy Assessor Josiah Rowe will take some homing pigeons to North Bloomfield and release them. Considerable money has been wagered on how long it takes for them to return.

Thieves entered the Nevada County quartz mill and scraped the plates. They got about $10 worth of gold.

In Washington, civil engineer Peary has been released from duty at the navel yard for five years leave to pursue arctic exploration.

Though late getting to it, 25 to 35 townspeople have formed a Fourth of July committee.

In Butte, a crime wave that ended in the cold-blooded shooting of William Kroaker has resurrected the Vigilantes.

Due to city finances, the position of night watchman will be eliminated June 1st.

William Burroughs, the morphine fiend, probably will serve time in the county boardinghouse.

Talk going around again about building a railroad from Nevada City to Marysville. Some feel that if the narrow gauge had been built to Marysville instead of Colfax, the valley town would never have complained about the hydraulic mining, causing the shutdown of same.

"I see your wife's cake took a prize at the fair," said one man. "When are you going to cut it?"

"Couldn't cut it with an axe," said the other man. "Same cake's won eight years in a row. It's like cement."

END

Jerry Goodwin

JEREMIAH GOODWIN

The Murderous Miner

by

Brad Prowse

In the California gold towns of You-Bet (U-Bet) and Red Dog, Jeremiah Goodwin was considered a friendly, prosperous, mining man. And so he was. But to the three men who died looking over the sights of his gun—four, if you count Goodwin's own death—he may have been something else altogether. Indeed, the record paints a Jekyll-Hyde portrait of this sometimes volatile man.

Jeremiah S. Goodwin—Jerry to his friends—was born in Stetson, Maine in 1852 so when he arrived in California in 1874, the Gold Rush was long over. Gold was now wrested from the earth either by hard rock mining or by using monitors, huge water cannons that tore down entire hills so the gold could be washed from the debris.

In Maine, Goodwin had been a farmer and blacksmith. But a little over a half year after settling in You-Bet, he was familiar enough with mining work that his company, the Bird's Eye Creek Company, sent him to Oregon to help fit up some mines they had there. Seven months later he returned to You-Bet and was made supervisor of the Neece and West Hydraulic Mines. Over the next thirty years Goodwin managed several mines, among them his own holdings, the Goodwin Gravel Mine and the Goodwin Drift Mine. He was a member of the IOOF and was generally well-liked and respected. But maybe there was a side to Goodwin that not everyone saw. If so, it might have come out shortly after the anti-debris laws were passed in the early 1880s.

Hydraulic mining was quite profitable but it was an ecological disaster. The water monitors washed away entire hillsides and sent them down water courses to the valley below. There, as the years wore on, the beds of the great valley rivers—the Sacramento, the American, the Yuba—began to fill with silt. At the least amount of winter drainage, these rivers could spill their banks, inundating cities, towns and farms. The capitol city of Sacramento itself had to raise the entire town by two stories to escape floods.

Finally, the farmers exercised their political muscle and shut down the hydraulic mines...well, almost. Some miners fought back. A telephone line twenty miles long was strung between the foothill town of Smartsville and the diggings at North Bloomfield.

When their man stationed in Smartsville spied government men heading that way to inspect the close-down, they could be warned to stop operations via the phone line. Unaware they were making history, the miners established the nation's first long distance phone line to thwart the law.

Goodwin also resisted the shutting down of the monitors, only he used another method. During the day he kept a 'care-taker' staff about the diggings. Come nightfall, he had his full crew out, washing down the hills.

Goodwin was also known to go armed with a pistol stuck in each back pocket. Then, around 1902, Goodwin suffered some paralysis from a stroke. It left him with an impaired limb and friends and acquaintances noted a definite change of attitude in the man. Well respected, yes. Liked, generally. But there was something about the man...

In 1903, Goodwin was living in the fine, big house he owned in You-Bet. One of his neighbors was Thomas Blue. Blue had come to the area in 1855 and himself built a reputation of some stature. A Democrat, in 1876 he served in the state assembly. His land—where he resided with his sons—abutted Goodwin's. Around 8 AM on April 23, 1903, Goodwin sent a Chinese laborer, Aw Bow, out to dig a water ditch on a section of his property to be used in working the land. This ditch was near where Blue's land joined Goodwin's.

Seeing the Chinese man working away with spade and pitchfork, Blue charged out and made the man stop working. The Chinese, who didn't speak or understand much English, retired to Goodwin's and indicated what had happened. Goodwin left his house and headed for the property line. In his pocket was a pistol—a rarity in those parts, one of the new automatics that had been on the market for only a few years.

At this point, several versions of what happened are recorded. The most accepted one—the one espoused by Goodwin—was that Blue, his nineteen-year old son, William, beside him, had cursed him, telling him that he couldn't dig the ditch, even if it was on his property. Goodwin tried to mollify Blue by suggesting they settle the dispute in court.

At this point, Blue advanced on Goodwin, striking him with a club and breaking his forearm. Goodwin continued to retreat another 30 or 40 yards when he was struck again by Blue and driven to the ground. As Blue moved in to continue the attack, Blue's son started to pick up a large rock, to smash Goodwin's head with.

Goodwin drew his pistol and shot the elder Blue three times and his son another three. Blue died instantly. His son, William, was mortally wounded, shot through the lungs.

Goodwin got up and headed for his house. On the way he was met by L. E. Linder, another neighbor. Goodwin went to Linder's home and then Linder went to check on the Blues. Thomas Blue was dead but William was still alive. A telephone message was sent to Nevada City, about eight miles away, and a Doctor Tickell came out at once.

Goodwin headed for Nevada City, the county seat, to turn himself in. Along the way, he was met by Under-Sheriff Waters to whom Goodwin surrendered. Once in town, a Dr. Muller found that Goodwin had a fractured left arm and a head injury.

Goodwin testified that Aw Bow came to him after he had been interrupted in digging the ditch. "He (Aw Bow) obeyed the (Blue's) order because their attitude was a threatening one," Goodwin said.

In one of Nevada County's more celebrated trails, several more shadings of the story came out. In a disposition made before he died the next day, William Blue said that it was Goodwin who had cursed his father and that no mention of legal arbitration was spoken of. Further, his father had a cane, perhaps one inch in diameter, not a club and he, the son, had not picked up a rock.

Porter Blue, a younger son, testified that he had observed the action from the Blue home, 200 feet away, and said he heard Goodwin curse his father. He said his brother did not try to strike Goodwin. There was some question raised as to whether Porter had been at the house or at the family well, as he had earlier claimed.

For Goodwin's side, a Miss Nettie Harris testified she was in Goodwin's house at the time of the shooting. She said she also had seen the attack and described it as taking place like Goodwin said. After the attack, she ran to the Linder home and notified Linder of the shooting.

Aw Bow, the laborer, while he couldn't understand the exchange between Goodwin and Blue, through a translator collaborated most of what Goodwin said. The main point was he stated that Blue started to strike Goodwin first.

Not helping the Blue's story was testimony made by Blue's granddaughter, Helen Kuffel, that she had heard her grandfather say earlier that morning that he intended to kill Goodwin. In the end, Judge George Coughlan found Goodwin not guilty in Thomas Blue's death. In a second trail over William's death, Goodwin was likewise cleared and the verdicts were generally held to have been fair.

But the double killings seemed to have affected Goodwin. In the ensuing years be became paranoid and continued to go armed. He complained about business failures and seemed worried about finances. These included land holdings, mining interests and 850 shares of stock in the Lyman Gilmore Airship Company, a local concern headed up by Lyman Gilmore who claimed he had flown before the Wright Brothers—only he could never prove it.

Le Roy Marden Clark, 40, was a foremen of one of Goodwin's properties. A quiet, unassuming man and well-liked, he was also a director of the Gilmore Airship Co. He and his wife had previously resided in Nevada City but now lived in one of the rooms in Goodwin's big house. The Clarks often looked after Goodwin during his bouts with Jim Beam and, thanks to Mrs. Clark's influence, Goodwin converted to Catholicism.

In the first few days of March, 1913, Mrs. Clark noted that Goodwin was acting strange. For instance, he went to Nevada City to purchase ammunition for his automatic. He took pains to leave the ammunition out on a table where Mrs. Clark could see it, an act that alarmed her. On March 3rd, Goodwin cleaned up his desk and put his safe and other papers into order, something he seldom did. Mrs. Clark thought this unusual—it was as if he was preparing for something to happen. He also had been drinking at a local saloon that day and was quite morose.

That same day, a You-Bet school teacher, Hazel Stennett, was sitting in a parlor just off Goodwin's bedroom. At the time, Goodwin was laying on his bed and he called out to her, pointing to a picture hanging on the wall. It was of Goodwin as a young man. He remarked how handsome he had looked then. Suddenly, without warning, he emptied his pistol into the picture!

Terrorized, Miss Stennett left the house and found Mrs. Clark. Afraid to reenter the house, they waited until Mr. Clark returned. Clark went in and got some warm clothing for the two women. They all then waited outside for awhile until Clark went in again and found Goodwin asleep.

He told the women to go to the Clark's room and lock the door. As soon as he had fed the animals, he would return.

(Another newspaper account said Mrs. Clark and Miss Stennett went directly to the Clark's room and does not mention the part about Clark finding them outside and his getting them warm clothes).

Possibly awakened by the opening of the barn door or a light there from a lantern, (it was near 8 PM) Goodwin realized Clark was home. He went to the Clark's bedroom door where he attempted to break it down. Clark, still outside, heard the commotion and ran to his wife's aid.

Again, the story enters the realm of conjecture. Since the door was closed, the women could only relate what they heard.

"What are you doing by my wife's bedroom door?" one of the women heard Clark cry out. Next there was a sound, much like a scuffle. Then, Mrs. Clark said she heard her husband say, "Give me your gun, Jerry!"

This was quickly punctuated by a shot, most likely from Goodwin's pistol, followed by a volley from both men. In the silence that followed, Mrs. Clark opened the door. Her husband reeled in, calling out, "I'm done for!" Shot through the heart, he still managed to make it to the bed where he died.

Miss Stennett stepped out into the death room. There, Goodwin lay. She had to step over him to get to a phone to call for a doctor, not knowing both men now were dead.

An examination of the shooting scene showed that the two men had been about ten feet apart. Since a large, ornate table with a Victrola on it in the middle of the room was not disturbed, there was some doubt as to a scuffle having taken place, though Goodwin had a gash in his head that might have come from a pistol blow.

Clark had been armed with a Colt .38 and he had fired three times, hitting Goodwin with each shot. Goodwin had fired his automatic 8 times, hitting Clark with four shots. The automatic pistol pound in Goodwin's hand had a full clip.

A search of the room turned up the empty pistol, flung aside when Goodwin reached for the second, loaded weapon. Both men received gunshots that should have been instantly fatal, yet Clark managed to stagger to his bed and Goodwin was able to draw a second gun before death overtook either man.

What was actually going through Goodwin's head those final days? Who knows? It was said he was worried about business finances. One report said that his estate was worth only about $300. But his two sisters and two nephews later petitioned to take over the estate and they valued it at $46,000.

There must have been some value to the estate because in 1916, Nahum (Nahenn) Goodwin, Jeremiah's brother, turned over all his rights to his brother's estate in lieu of $1500 to purchase a piece of property to be used as a life-estate, $5,000 for livestock for said property, and an $8000 annuity, the interest on which he could draw as long as he lived—and he lived until 1930. Twenty-five hundred dollars was also set aside to pay all his other debts—excluding his liquor bills run up in local taverns.

Goodwin was buried in the nearby Red Dog cemetery, his final resting spot unknown as any headstone or marker has long since vanished. Along with it vanished any knowledge there might have been of the private demons that drove Goodwin to carry a brace of pistols that he was more than ready use.

END

100 YEARS AGO IN NEVADA COUNTY

November, 1897

by

Brad Prowse

James Wise was the man who stole Cap Vaughn's overcoat and shoes last month. Sixty days, says the judge (thirty extra for the shoes).

Thomas Evens killed Robert Holland on the Spanish Mine Road by driving a miner's candlestick through Holland's eye. Evens said it was self defense. Despite his claim, angry crowds fill the streets and the sheriff has taken precautions against lynching.

Rehearsal for the operetta, Trail By Jury, is being held at Miss Renfroe's studio at eight.

Weather clear on the third.

The Malakoff mine has resumed work and North Bloomfield hopes to prosper.

A lady's baseball team is being organized.

We learn that Frank J. Gross shot his nephew, Frank E. Gross of Rough and Ready, in cold blood, not in a gunfight as earlier reported.

Mr. and Mrs. Dunkley suffered the loss of their son, Palmer, to diphtheria.

Showers on the seventh and eighth.

Miss Maude Heath has been appointed telephone operator of French Corral.

Miss Gertie Lord, who left Grass Valley to pursue a career on stage, died in Cincinnati from taking carbolic acid. The third of three sisters to die by their own hand, she was despondent over the life she was living.

The Episcopal Fair at McDonald's Hall was a big success.

George Turner's horse ran away, destroying harness and vehicle.

James Bottomely of Red Dog, one of the area's oldest pioneers, is near death at 83.

Water sales for October were $1,011. Amount delinquent, $1,130.

Germany has seized a Chinese seaport under the pretext of the deaths of two German citizens in that country. China is a good example of a country without a strong government or army. Vast, ponderous and unorganized, it would be best if China was partitioned among nations that would give it strong law and government. Carve the possum!

Stormy near mid-month. Rainfall to date: 11.37 inches.

Joe Flynn got a badly mashed toe in a cave-in at the Maryland Mine.

Two men were forcing a team to draw a heavy load up Banner Hill when one threatened to beat the horses with a club. Don Luddington stopped the man. We need to have an SPCA chapter here.

Nancy Allison McKinley, the President's mother, has died.

Henry Shivley, of Moores Flat, had his arrest warrant against George Conley thrown out as he presented no evidence. Many think that China brandy was the prime mover in the case.

Fair weather again.

The House passed a bill to appropriate $175,000 for relief of starving miners in the Yukon.

Donation Day coming. Don't forget your potato and stick of wood.

A fight between Beckman, the German Cyclone and Gilmore, the Wonder of Woods Ravine, will be held tonight—$50 purse.

Carolers are beginning to be seen on the streets.

Union barber shops will stay open until eight Friday evening and close at noon on Christmas Day.

A big crowd is expected for the football game on Christmas Day.

The Union circulation nears 2000.

William Luckey, M. McGuire, and Samuel Collins had a row with John Haier last night. Haier got a revolver and defied them all.

Constable Scott of Nevada City has petitioned the Government for compensation of his service in the Piute War of 1860, so far, without avail.

Annie McCabe, twenty-five, is lodged in the county jail for common drunkenness. A sad case, her condition is said to have started after a bout of typhoid three years ago.

Nevada City is rated one of the best 'show towns' on the coast but until Grass Valley builds its own theater, we can't expect many first class attractions here.

Since San Francisco and other large California cities are banning boxing, Sheriff Getchell said there will be no more prizefights locally lest the area be overrun with fights and the riff-raff they bring.

The iron steamer Cleveland, from Seattle, was wrecked off Vancouver and most of her crew has been lost.

The County Hotel boasts a good sextet of singers. Many enjoyed their renditions of 'Where Is My wandering Boy Tonight,' 'Home Sweet Home,' 'Nearer My God To Thee' and 'A Flower From Mother's Grave.' During today's concert, when 'Where Is My Wandering Boy,' ended, a brakeman from Truckee, jailed for stealing a bible, called out, 'Locked up safe in the Nevada County Jail, you blankety-blanks!'

The Truckite was taken to the kitchen, his head under the sink hydrant for five minutes and his mouth filled with brown soap.

Mrs. George Zink, who lives on the North San Juan Road, is dangerously ill from inflammation of the bowels.

After the 14th of January, keno and around-the-table-poker will be illegal in Nevada City.

FATHER: Are you sure your love for my daughter is the genuine article.

SUITOR: It is not possible for me to be mistaken, sir. I've had the feeling a thousand times.

GENTELMEN, CHOOSE YOUR WEAPONS;

PISTOLS, RIFLES OR WATERHOSE

Dueling in the California Mining Camps

by

Brad Prowse

Two men glower at each other across the 25 paces separating them. Each holds a fully loaded Colt's revolver in one hand and, at a signal, both open fire, advancing as they shoot. Lead and great billows of white, sulfurous smoke fill the air. But when the sounds of the shots die away and the pistols are empty, both antagonists still stand, unharmed. In sheer frustration, one man raises his revolver above his head and charges, finally bringing the other man down with a well placed clout to the head.

Thus was honor vindicated in the mining camp of North Bloomfield, California one fine autumn day in 1866 between two Frenchmen, Souchet and Picard—no first names surviving from the account of the duel, even if they did.

Dueling wasn't an unusual occurrence in the rough and relatively primitive conditions of California's mining camps. A general lack of formal legal proceedings, a high percentage of young, quick-tempered males and the casual wearing of firearms, made dueling a popular method of settling accounts. These affairs, however, due to the fun-loving spirit that infested the camps, sometimes turned out to be more ludicrous than deadly.

A duel that saw much liquid spilled, but none of it red, took place between two Nevada City citizens in 1861. A Messrs. Tompkins and Curley, again, no first names survive, became offended of one another for some reason and a challenge was made. Perhaps because it was a hot July day, the weapons chosen weren't pistols but water hoses.

Two 25 foot sections of fire hose with quarter-inch nozzles were hooked up to separate hydrants, each hydrant being backed by 150 pounds of water pressure. Strong columns of water blasted each man about the streets, knocking first one contestant and then another down into the mud, mire and horse droppings. But neither man would give quarter and the duel ended only after one of the hose burst.

Though no blood was let, the great quantities of water spilled seemed to suffice and the duel ended on a friendly note.

In the Sierra mining town of Cherokee, on Christmas Eve, 1874, two men attending a Christmas ball got into an argument over the affections of a young lady who was present. Again, names are scarce. One man was remembered only as 'The Cherokee blacksmith' and the other was simply called 'Wall.' In any case, words were spoken, insults traded and Christmas morning found both men with loaded pistols and 30 feet between them. The signal came and the blacksmith quickly fired before Wall had fully raised his pistol. Finding himself unharmed, Wall magnanimously fired his pistol into the air and advanced, his hand extended in friendship. The duel was ended, no harm was done and the two men swore lifelong devotion towards each other. What they didn't know, until later, was that the blacksmith had about as much chance of hitting Wall with his shot as Wall had of hitting the moon with his. The seconds had loaded the guns with blank charges.

Pistols contained their full compliment of lead, though, in the duel fought between Canadian Jim Lundy and George Dibble, a graduate of Annapolis. A dispute over a mining claim on the Yuba River near Nevada City—and an epithet uttered by Lundy—caused Dibble to issue a challenge.

Lundy was a large, bullying man, though capable of showing the white feather. He had one eye—the other lost to a man he tried to cow—and was known as a dead shot. Dibble's friends tried to talk him out of his going through with the duel but without avail.

The challenge was accepted and Colt's pistols at 15 paces were selected. The duel was fought on November 1, 1851 with General J. C. Morehead acting as Dibble's second, C. E. G. Morse as Lundy's. Before the duel, Lundy was said to have indicated on Dibble's breast where he intended to shoot the man.

The two men took their stations and Lundy, true to his nature, fired before the word was given, hitting Dribble where he said he would. Dibble threw down his pistol, said "You fired too soon," walked a short distance and fell to the ground and died. Lundy was tried twice for the crime but in neither case could a conviction be obtained.

Justice of a sort was done when, some years later, Lundy, drunk to the nines, climbed to his hotel room in a Sonora hotel. A fire broke out and Lundy, unaware in his drunken stupor, was overlooked in the resultant confusion. The following day his skeleton was recovered from the ashes.

During a campaign against some Indians in 1860 a number of Nevada County, California men joined the Nevada Rifles to fight in that state. Some difficulty between Captain J. B. Van Hagan of the Rifles and a Nevada County volunteer, R. B. Moyes came up. Moyes vowed to settle matters 'when this cruel war is over.' He kept his pledge by issuing a challenge to the Captain when the company, covered with glory and dust, finally returned to camp.

Van Hagan chose rifled muskets at 60 paces and on June 20th, 1860, the two men faced off near Grizzly Flat, California, to settle accounts. The two blazed away but without noticeable effect. While some wag suggested putting telescopes on the rifles, the two men demanded a second go and the rifles were loaded again. Once more the muzzle loaders roared, smoke rolled out in great clouds...and no one was hit. A 'big talk' was then held which resulted in a peaceful settlement and both heroes were spared for future deeds of valor.

Another duel that put a lot of lead in the air but produced little more effect than the foregoing, took place in Nevada City in 1853. The cause of the dispute was rooted in the fiery passions of pre-Civil War politics. Billy Mason, an unsuccessful candidate for the state assembly, blamed his defeat on H. C. Gardiner, a man who had worked against Mason's election.

Mason confronted Gardiner in a hotel bar one evening and proceeded to threaten him with a pistol and a great deal of invective. Gardiner allowed as how he was unarmed at the moment, but that he would be glad to oblige Mason at any convenient time. The city streets, at nine the next morning, seemed mutually agreeable and the men parted.

At around nine the next day Gardiner borrowed a 'Navy pistol,' probably a Colt's .36 caliber revolver, and went looking for Mason. The latter saw Gardiner first and opened up on him from the cover of a narrow alley. Gardiner took a shot in the calf of the leg but stood his ground in the open, firing occasionally at the almost hidden Mason who still blasted away from time to time. Mason got a bit careless at one point and received a wound in his leg quite similar to the one inflicted on Gardiner.

Both men finally emptied their revolvers and the onlookers to the fray, hidden until now, ran out and stopped the bloodletting. On checking around, it was discovered that besides the slight wounds each man took, a small pig, running loose in the streets had been hit by a stray bullet. Alas, the porker was dead. The next day someone was spreading the word that a pig and two calves had been shot. In any case, no further action was taken by either duelist and Mason lost considerable face for his conduct in the fray.

A duel with Colt's 'six-shooters,' as the newspaper account reported, took place just outside Downieville in 1852. John Kelly and William Spear—the latter one of the first members of the Sierra County bar—were friends, often ribbing each other in the manly atmosphere of the early-day mining camp. But, unfortunately, both became enamored of the same woman and they had a falling out.

Friends of the two men tried to settle the problem of which man should enjoy the exclusive favors of the young `lady' but neither man would budge and Kelly challenged Spear to meet on the field of honor. Kelly wanted to settle the argument with fists but Spear—who was the challenged man—insisted on revolvers.

The two men—along with seconds, a doctor, the disputed damsel and a good portion of the town, retired to Sportsman's Flat, a mile above Downieville on the Yuba River. The two men were put into position while the onlookers emphasized their deep concern for the participants by wagering nearly $3000 on the outcome. The rules of the contest were simple: At the command of `Fire,' both men were free to unload their revolvers at each other until one was disabled or called for a cessation of hostilities.

At the cry, `Fire,' both men touched off a cap—to no avail—both still stood. Spear immediately recocked his revolver and took aim for a second shot but Kelly's gun jammed. Spear's Colt went off again and once more Kelly found himself miraculously untouched—but with a weapon that still would not fire.

Spear was just lining up his sights for a third try at Kelly, struggling with his broken gun when the man, too game to run but agitated beyond standing still any longer, suddenly charged Spear, flinging the disabled revolver at him. Spear, unnerved, dropped his weapon and took off at a run.

In short order he was captured by the crowd and brought back where the two men shook hands and Spear agreed the that the fair charmer should be Kelly's. Later it leaked out that the seconds had loaded the guns with powder and wad—but no pistol balls.

But gold country duels weren't always matters of horseplay, or, at worse, a little minor bloodshed. They could be every bit as earnest and deadly as any French field of honor ever thought of being.

Andy Fugate and Jack White were two of the lesser desperados that hung around the High Sierra railroad town of Truckee, California in the early days, making their livings doing as little honest work as possible. Though both were outlaws, considerable bad blood existed between the two men, apparently due to some disagreement over a woman, probably a soiled dove in the rail town's Street of Shame.

On the night of September 5th, 1873, the duo happened to meet on Front Street. Fugate inquired of White if he was `heeled,' to which White answered "Yes," acknowledging that he was properly festooned with the requisite sidearm. Evidently this was the answer Fugate was waiting for because he suddenly went for his own artillery.

As bystanders and evening strollers dove into alleyways or dropped down behind horse troughs, bullets whizzed through the air and, after a few practice shots for range, into the erstwhile gunslingers. Fugate managed to shoot White down then walked up to the badly wounded man, thumbed back the hammer of his revolver and casually shot him several more times as he lay in the street.

But White, with superhuman effort, was able to raise himself up and pump three bullets of his own into Fugate. Possessed with the rage and desperation of wild animals, both men continued to hold their positions, snapping away at each other with empty pistols until both fell dead.

The coming of law and order, the enforcement of the codes against dueling and the influence of civilization all helped to bring an end to the practice of two men settling their differences over the sights of a brace of pistols. For whether it was done with the tongue-in-cheek attitude of a broad farce or with deadly intent, using fully loaded revolvers at suicidal range, dueling was decreed to be only another form of murder.

END

100 YEARS AGO

IN NEVADA COUNTY

MARCH 1898

by

Brad Prowse

Miss Hackley is teaching Miss Esther Hogden's class while the latter is ill.

Word on the Maine is that the explosion came from the outside—possibly a torpedo.

March has been unsettled—clouds, light rain and fair, cold nights.

The cottage at the Empire Mine used by Robert Walker and family is about to undergo enlargement.

Richard Kissinger was discharged from a Tin Plate works in Philadelphia for kissing a woman employee. The union is up in arms but the woman has not complained.

Thomas Evans, convicted of killing Ron Holland, will be in court today to face a life sentence.

The Rector brothers planted some maples in the National Hotel annex but they were torn up by some miserable wretch. Such miscreants should be in jail.

An unusual amount of sickness in town, particularly influenza and bad colds.

Teddy O'Neal got 20 days for indecent exposure.

There's a social dance at the Union Hall in Indian Flat tomorrow night.

New uniforms for the National Guard have arrived. Company I will soon be togged up in fine shape.

A dried fish of immense size was the attraction at the Union Food Store yesterday.

Spain is buying warships and a fresh squadron is readying to sail for Cuba.

Miners at Manzanita Diggings discovered Toy Duck working their sluice. After catching him again, he was arrested—ten days.

The Navy's negotiating to buy warships in preparation of possible hostilities while the Illinois National Guard is prepared to ship 7500 men and 4000 latest pattern .45 caliber Springfield rifles east.

Moores Flat and Granitville will soon have telephones.

A special train took 60 Chinese from Nevada City to Grass Valley where they elected a joss.

Payday at most of the mines will mean $35,000 put into circulation.

Nineteen lives lost in a Skaguay hotel fire.

The G.A.R. parade Wednesday will be one of the largest seen in these parts.

Grass Valley consumes more than 300 tons of coal a month.

Mrs. Mary Calmes, a member of the Donnor Party, died in Oakland.

The notorious murderer, Indian Dick, was shot while resisting arrest. This brings great relief to the citizens of Squaw Valley, who he terrorized.

Phil Scadden's grocery store now sports a glass-front cracker counter.

John Marsh fell 25 feet in the Merrifield Mine when a ladder broke. He narrowly escaped death.

In Kentucky, two Negroes will be sold into slavery, the first since 1865. They have been repeatedly convicted of vagrancy and the county is selling their services for the time of conviction. Whoever buys them must house and clothe them and use their labor in any way they see fit.

Lack of rain has the mine owners worried as most depend on water to power their machinery.

Ladies passing along Pine Street near the Glenbrook Saloon complained of vile and disgraceful language used by a drunken man. Measures should be taken to prevent such profanity on the streets.

Spain has dispatched a torpedo flotilla to Puerto Rico as war talk heightens.

W.H. Freeman has a new delivery wagon and it's a daisy.

A party of Digger Indians passed through town yesterday.

The next few days will determine peace or war. The President feels conflict may yet be averted.

Three teenage girls were drunk on the streets last night. All have good homes and it's believed young men gave them the liquor. The girls were warned and evidence gained against the men. Such offenses are becoming more prevalent and measures will be taken against them.

L. Paine is down from Lake City.

Wagons driven by steam engines will soon replace mules to haul Borax out of Nevada mines.

Milkman Towle's horse ran away and smashed a wheel at Pine and Commercial.

Mrs. John Treanor of Sacramento Street swore out a warrant against Fred Timm for pointing a pistol at her. Timm claimed that when he got home that morning, he found Treanor in his bed and told her to leave.

E. G. (Ned) Withington, the carriage and sign painter, has lived here since 1849.

Assistant Secretary of the Navy, Theodore Roosevelt, has urged intervention in Cuba.

Policemen went to Fred Timm's cabin to arrest him for threatening Mrs. Treanor's life where they found them having a `free and easy' time. Both were placed in nippers and hauled in.

The 35th regiment of colored troops, along with Lt. Lyman Welch of Nevada City, was ordered to leave Montana for Florida.

A sign of age in a woman is when she gets out of a buggy backwards.

**Old hard-rock miner, Bill corin, shortly before
his death at 91 in 1999. he holds a picture of his old mining
shift, of which, he was the last living member.**

**Mine mule. Most mines used mules to haul
oarcarts. Once in the mine, they never saw daylight again.**

BILL CORIN

by

Brad Prowse

"I figured out a neat way high-grade gold out of the mine," Bill Corin said, leaning over his kitchen table, nursing a cigarette. "I had these little pockets sewn to my undershorts that I could fill with gold. Then I tied them down to make them lay flat under my clothes. My wife, Madeline, sewed some extra cloth to the bottom of my undershirt so it would cover the shorts when we were in the change room, changing out of our mine clothes to leave."

"One day after work, when I was heading for where my wife was waiting with the car, one of the ties came loose and the little pocket shot straight out. My wife yelled, `Bill! Can't you wait until you get home for that!'"

"I looked down and saw what she meant. `Shut up and get going,' I said, jumping in the car and worried a mine manager might see it. `It ain't what you think!'"

Bill Corin was born on January 30th, 1908, in Redruth, Cornwall, England. It wasn't an easy life. By the time he was three, his father had died of silicosis from working in the Cornwall tin mines. By the age of 14, Bill was doing a man's work in the mines himself. In 1925, Bill emigrated to Canada, ending up in Timmons, Onterio, underground again in the Hollinger gold mine.

"It was awful cold up there," Bill remembers. "A man could read the papers by the Northern Lights in the winter, they were so bright.

Bill heard that men for underground mining—hard-rock mining—were needed in the mines of Nevada County, California, where it was a lot warmer. So, in 1930, he packed his kit and headed south.

California's gold country is extensive and traces of the precious metal have turned up almost everywhere in the state. But the greatest concentration turned out to be in the Mother Lode—the area of the original strike in 1848—and the Northern Mines Area, north of the Mother Lode.

The Mother Lode, so long heralded in stories by Bret Harte, Mark Twain and others, stretched—roughly—from just north of Yosemite Park to about the town of Auburn, some 30 miles east of Sacramento. The Northern

Mines covered the area from Auburn to around Downieville, in the Sierra Nevada foothills.

While men were searching for gold in the northern area within a year of the original strike in 1848, near Coloma, it is sometimes overlooked by the history buff or the tourist seeking signs of the old camps and diggin's.' As a matter of fact, the Northern Mines proved to be richer than the Mother Lode and the area still contains a number of small mining operations.

"I went to work at the Empire Mine in Grass Valley," Bill said. "It's been turned into a park, now, but in them days, there was two eight-hour shifts runnin,' six days a week."

Bill started out as a mucker—a man who operates that ancient machine, the shovel—and then moved up to be a miner, a timberman and finally a powderman. A miner was the one who drilled the holes, a powderman loaded them and set them off and a timberman did his best to keep the whole thing from coming down on everyone's head.

The pay wasn't great but—especially in those depression years—it was steady. "Muckers made $3.00 a day, miners $3.50 and timbermen and powdermen, $4.25," said Bill. "And that was in gold coin—at least until Roosevelt stepped in and took the country off the Gold Standard. It was paper money after that."

In any case, Nevada County's twin gold towns of Grass Valley and Nevada City knew no want.

"All the drillin' was done with air," Bill remembers. "Sometimes a man was standin' on a pile of quartz ore with twenty feet above him. Other times, he was layin' on his side, workin' in no more than three feet a' space. It was damp, wet work, about 60 degrees most of the time."

There are several major ways to get gold out of the ground, most very labor intensive. In the earliest days, it was possible to actually pick nuggets out of the streams—this was the easy way to get gold and probably the origin of the rumor that 'gold was there just for the picking up.' It was, but not for long. The influx of men into the gold fields soon exhausted that source. Now to get more gold, it was the miners who themselves would be exhausted.

Panning, sluice boxes and water monitors (until 1884 when they were outlawed because they were filling up the rivers in the valley below with debris) were the above-ground methods. Panning was usually reserved for checking out an area for color. Once it was established there was a reasonable amount of gold, sluice boxes (long toms) were constructed, long wooden troughs with riffles built into the bottom to catch the gold. Water was run down the box, gravel shoveled in, and the washing process—

sometimes helped along by rocking the sluice box, would yield up the gold—if the miners were lucky.

Monitor were huge water hoses, supplied with copious amounts of water brought in by ditch. Their method of use was simple—point the monitor at a likely looking hill and wash it away! As the debris came down off the hillsides, it was processed for gold—though this was wasteful method and a lot of finer gold got past the process. It also filled the riverbeds of the waterways in the valley, causing the residents there to build a series of dikes and levees to contain them. To this day it still causes them much grief. The hardest physical way to get the gold was to go in after it—drilling, blasting, mucking out and drilling some more. This was hard-rock mining.

Hard-rock mining went something like this: Once a likely vein of gold was found, drilling into the indigenous rock began, the men following the vein of gold. If the vein went up down or sideways, so did the tunnel. Most mines had to start digging downward at some point. Sometimes a straight shaft was dug, served by an elevator. Other times the shaft was at an angle and a `skip,' a long cart that could transport men, machinery, supplies and ore, would be used to move things up and down the shaft.

At spots were a likely vein was found, a `station' would be established. Here the elevator or skip would off-load men and material so the vein could be worked. Nearby would be a place to pile the ore as it awaited a trip to the surface and on to the mills. Drifts were dug, following the veins, usually five or so feet wide and about seven feet high. Raises might be run upward, following the veins. These would be timbered as needed. As the raises in a location became more numerous, they would become connected, forming one large area or `stope' that had been worked and excavated of material.

This is just an example of a system that was far more complex in practice. The Empire mine itself went to 4,600 feet, then, after a mile walk on the horizontal, dropped to 6,000.

"Machinery lifted the skips and elevators but down in the mine, the ore carts were pulled by mules," Bill said. "These animals were lowered in slings and spent their whole lives underground from then on. If one ever had to be taken out, you had to shield its eyes—they couldn't take the bright sun."

Working in the mines was dangerous but Bill remembers only two fatalities—both due to cave-ins.

"There were rats in the mine," Bill said. "We'd feed them scraps from our lunches. And we kept an eye on them while we worked. If the rats suddenly disappeared, we got out, fast. Just dropped everything and ran. The rats could tell it before we could—a cave-in was coming." "We had carbide lamps on our helmets. Even if they went out, we could find our way to a skip," Bill said. "All you had to do was put one foot into the water trench that ran along the right side of the tunnel and the other on a rail. They'd take you out."

The mines smelled of powder gas, machine oil and wet timbers. Perhaps the most deadly danger was a silent one—silicosis, the disease of the lungs that came from breathing all the rock dust.

Bill was a family man—in spades. He was wed six times and has three daughters. A widower four times, his last wife divorced him in 1976.

"Lots of miners were single men, though," Bill said. "That's why Grass Valley had a lot of 'houses' in them days. One of the biggest was on Main Street—right across from the City Hall."

During the war, the mines were shut down and Bill found himself with the 116th Combat Engineers in the South Pacific—as a demolition and explosives man. He was sent to Australia, Borneo, the Dutch East Indies and the Philippines. Then a stray shell—perhaps a mortar round—put him in Letterman Army Hospital in San Francisco and out of the war.

After the war he returned to the Empire—but this time he stayed topside, seeing to the pumps that kept the mine dry.

"Working with the pumps," Bill said. "Sure put a crimp in the chances to high-grade."

High-grades was the taking of ore from the mine without bothering to pass it through management's hands. Everybody who could did it and the mine owners knew it. It was a small but nagging drain on their profits and there was a constant battle of ingenuity between the miners and the owners over high-grades.

"High-grade was gold specimens, almost pure gold," Bill said. "Might be nuggets, might be quartz shot full of gold. Miner run across a bunch of it, was a big temptation to take a little for hisself."

"Finding the ore wasn't so hard. Gettin' it out'a the mine, that took some thought," Bill said. "One way was to put it in your lunch pail and before it was checked on the way out, try to make a swap with someone else who already had been checked."

"Some men put a chunk in their mouth. Was an unspoken rule—you never clapped a man on the back as you left the mine. Might make him choke to death on a nugget."

"And wasn't supposed to knock a man's dirty clothes out from under his arm at the end of the week, when he was taking them home to wash. Might be some ore wrapped up in them."

"'Course," Bill went on, "mine owners was pretty sharp, too. In one mine, the Idaho-Maryland, they made the men take showers after a shift.

Was later stopped when the law said they couldn't do that to them. And they could shake your lunch bucket, see if ore was rattling around inside.

"Fred Knobs was the mine manager. He'd been in mining a long time. Once worked with Herbert Hoover, back when he was a mining engineer. Anyway, if he saw a miner with a new car, he'd move him to a job where the man wasn't near any gold to high-grade. He figured a miner couldn't afford a new car on miner's wages so he must'a been high-grading."

"Back when gold was $20 an ounce," Bill said, "we could get about $15 for it. That was about three days pay."

Bill said that there were certain people in town who would buy high-grade or it could be taken to Marysville, a town in the valley about 30 mikes away, where a Chinese man would purchase it.

"A man could get maybe an ounce or so out at one time, he was careful," Bill said. "Maybe more, he had 'shorts' like mine. Only gold I have around today is this ring."

Bill put his fist forward and on one finger is a gold ring inset with a piece of quartz bearing a bright streak of gold across its face.

"That's gold from the old 16 to 1 Mine they're still working up near Allegheny—but I didn't get it by high-grade. Had to buy it."

"Sure wish I could get down into the Empire today," Bill said, wistfully. "About the 4200 foot level. I know where there's some high-grade worth— oh, today, about $8,000. If I could get to it, would pay for a nice trip back to Cornwall."

END

(This interview with Bill took place in 1998. Bill went back to minin' in 1999—but on the other side of the Pearly Gates).

ONE HUNDRED YEARS AGO

IN NEVADA COUNTY

July 1898

by

Brad Prowse

The sports committee has arranged for races and jumping on Mill and Main Streets for the Fourth; high jumps, potato and distance races and fire companies racing in heats.

In the slander case of George Gehrig vs. Simon Hieronimus, Gehrig was awarded one dollar.

Those singing in the chorus on the Fourth of July are requested to meet at Lord's Hall Saturday evening.

General Shafter has begun his attack against Spanish forces in Santiago.

Officer Dahlgren arrested Joseph Collinson and Frank Kuhlman for disturbing the peace.

Nevada City celebrated the Fourth with parades, marching bands, ranks of National Guard soldiers and hose and engine companies, along with minstrels and oratory—all ending with a fireman's ball that lasted until dawn.

Five hundred passengers and crew were lost when the French liner La Burgogne was run down by an iron sailing ship off Halifax.

Whenever a man is elected to office, he looks around for an assistant to do the work.

Aw Cue, the Chinese cook, was charged with stealing $80 from Phelan Sister's restaurant.

And the Chinese on upper Commercial Street have been uneasy due to a strange looking bearded Oriental who has been in their midst. They consider him a 'hoo-doo' and have been breathing easier since he left on the noon train yesterday.

The Stanford Mine is now being leased by Joseph Thomas.

Rankin and George Bayne were fined $10 each for battery committed on C. C. Ragsdale.

Washington claims Spain wishes an armistice.

Poundmaster Craig has been accused of driving cows from outside town into the pound. One man found his fence cut and had to pay $3.00 to retrieve the animal from the pound.

Miss Elizabeth Penrose of Relief hill died at home yesterday. She was 69.

Ballgame this afternoon at Watt Park between the Pioneers and the Banners.

Sam Gilliam's little boy was alighting from a wagon when the brake flew back, striking him and leaving a bad bruise on his head.

Pedestrians scattered when a horse and cart dashed down Boulder after being frightened by a boy sprinkling the streets. Several parked vehicles were damaged.

Henry Carrag's ranch at French Corral is for sale—376 acres, three room house, almond grove, 2 large barns—$1600.

Young Frank Ford of Boston Ravine was badly burned while playing with a toy cannon.

Elderly gentlemen seem to have a penchant for youngerly ladies.

General Torral surrendered Santiago. Spanish troops to be deported.

Deer and dove season has started.

A daring train robbery happened in the Truckee Division, just east of Humboldt, when two masked men held up train No. 1.

Some Chinese have purchased the Red Dog Mine.

W. G. Lord has a handsome new buggy. It has rubber tires and is easy riding.

Tin Loy, the Chinese merchant, passed away last evening. He came from China in the early '50s and was prominent in Grass Valley. His estate is estimated at $10,000. He took much pride in his daughter, Mrs. Lillie King Owyang, presently attending Cooper Medical College.

Joseph Phillips house was destroyed by fire. A lamp exploded.

General Miles is on route to Puerto Rico while Dewey prepares to bombard forts in Manila.

Teamsters are complaining about the bad roads near Sugar Loaf.

Pioneer E. O. Thompkins crossed the dark river yesterday after a long illness.

Thus far, $123,000,000 has been expended on the war. Killed in battle, 247.

Graniteville nights are delightfully cool compared with the day's heat.

Over a million feet of lumber has been cut at the Marsh mill this season.

The President says the U.S. does not want the Philippines and has no designs on them. Due to the hostility of the inhabitants, the islands would only be a problem to America.

Three houses on upper Pine in Nevada City burned. The heat from the Penrose home set an engine on fire and caused a horse to collapse.

Ninety-two at the courthouse and one hundred and twelve at the NCNGRR depot.

Bismark, former Chancellor of Germany, has died.

A successful doctor is one who can relieve his patients of good fees.

Charles Peters, 45, a stranger, hung himself in a Truckee barn. He was despondent over ill health.

Cigarettes are expected to contribute $3,000,000 a year to the war tax.

Deputy Sheriff Pascoe's holster broke on the road between Grass Valley and Glenbrook Park. His name is on the gun and he will be grateful for its return.

1st IRISHMAN: Poor Timmy. Foive years he got in Sing-Sing.

2nd IRISHMAN: Begorra, and yer sympathy is wasted! He's surrounded by friends!

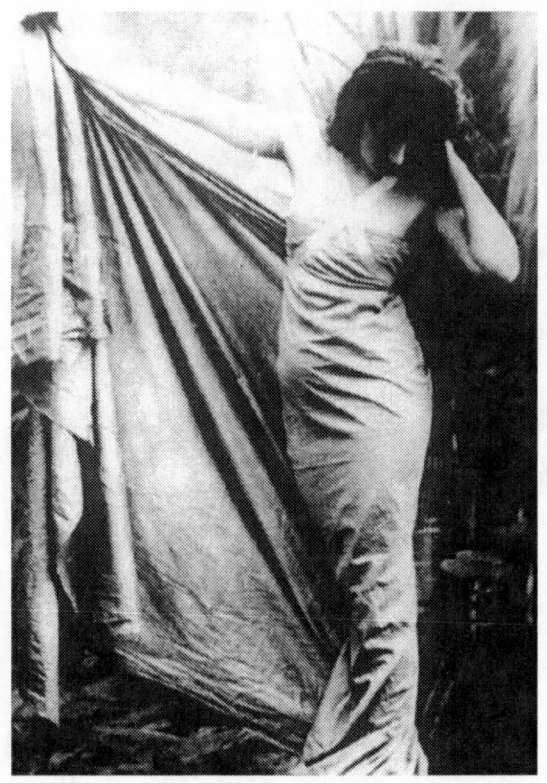

The Spring Chicken-amazingly svelte for the age she lived in.

Truckee in the 1890's

WHEN THE SPRING CHICKEN

HAD SHARP CLAWS

by

Brad Prowse

John Whipley had a bone to pick with George Prior. He finally tracked him to a saloon on Fourth Street in the rowdy railroad town of Truckee, California. Both men were heeled and after an exchange of gunfire, Whipley was heavier by three slugs in his lower regions and soon died while Prior would be crippled for life from a bullet in the shoulder.

If the gunplay and general murderous intent often exhibited in the early-day frontier towns was largely a masculine activity, it's probably safe to say much of it was engaged in over the affections of some woman. Certainly, the altercation between John Whipley and George Prior (or Pryor) was precipitated by the ardor Whipley felt toward one of Truckee's fairer Cyprians. But, after both men had put sufficient holes in each other, the ladies took matters into their own hands and extended the hostilities.

Truckee is plunked down, about 30 miles west of Reno, Nevada, just below the infamous pass named for the Donner Party, (who, thanks to deep snow, turned to dining upon one another). Early on a railroad town, besides the Sons of the Shining Steel, it also hosted miners and loggers—and very few women. It was, in other words, a gathering of virile, hard working, hard drinking and hard playing wage-earning males sans 'decent' women. This invited an influx of 'ladies of the evening' and the usual following of gamblers, gunmen and toughs. Two such were George Prior and John Whipley.

It seems that Prior's girlfriend, a young and beautiful—but extremely dangerous—woman named Carrie Smith, also called 'The Spring Chicken,' had a beef with one Belle Butler. On the 4th of July, 1869, Carrie, accompanied by her gallant, Prior, went to the 'establishment' of Lotta Morton where Belle 'worked.' Once there, she abused and threatened to kill Belle. This so distressed Belle, who was said to be a beautiful and intelligent lady despite her choice of callings, that Lotta's gentleman friend, John Whipley, agreed to take up her cause.

The next day, Whipley found Prior in the saloon on Truckee's Fourth Street and both men 'went to shooting.' Eight shots later, when the smoke had cleared away, Whipley was dying, having been hit in bowels and groin, and Prior had taken a slug in the shoulder and was permanently crippled.

Soon thereafter, Carrie went out to find a room for her wounded hero. While on the streets of Truckee, she ran into Lotta, recently bereft of her own man. There proceeded a hair-pulling, skin-scratching, screaming fight between the two members of the 'weaker set.'

Belle, who was nearby, decided to get in the fray and approached with a pistol pulled from somewhere. She placed the gun at Carrie's back and pulled the trigger. But the fair Carrie managed to shift position at that instant, trying to get a better hold of Lotta's black tresses, and the ball wounded Lotta instead. Thus ended the series.

Belle was sent to San Quentin for 18 months for her part in the altercation. Carrie, The Spring Chicken, went uncharged in this particular incident.

But Carrie was considered an extremely violent and dangerous young woman and was hauled before the local court at least twice in the next few years—both times for stabbings. On April 4th, 1873, she put a knife to James Fagan, leaving him bleeding in the city streets. That one cost her a $150. On January 7th, 1877, she held an encore using a one J.M. Linsom. Linsom also lived but probably he was a bit more selective of his feminine companionship from then on.

Carrie's exploits finally brought her to the attention of the '601,' Truckee's vigilante committee. It was said she openly defied them, claiming she could depend on the support of some forty 'roughs' to back her up. In any case, by the late 1870s, the 601 had cleaned up Truckee somewhat and Carrie, The Spring Chicken, either settled down to a peaceful roost or flew the coop altogether as her name doesn't seem to be attached to any further mayhem in the town after those days.

100 YEARS AGO IN NEVADA COUNTY

September 1899

by

Brad Prowse

The Grass Valley theater manager complains of the howling made by young boys during performances.

September has been dry, the hottest day of the year coming near month's end.

It's reported that an Edison phonograph has been hooked to a Bell telephone so that messages will be recorded when a person is not at home. We can't see much demand for such a contraption.

A fearful runaway in Nevada City. A four-horse team pulling a lumber wagon became frighten by sprinkler hoses on Commercial Street, dashed up to Pine, turned, with one horse going around a light pole and breaking away, then flew down Broad, the driver, Joaquin Lopez, standing in the box. He jumped out as the wagon crashed into another vehicle. Neither horses, wagons nor driver were badly hurt.

Apache Indians, chasing Zunis they claim killed some of their own, were stopped at Jerome and driven back to their reservation.

W. J. Steven's little son is ill with tonsillitis and Mrs. Etta Gassaway has typhoid-malarial fever.

Joe Awk claims he was fleeced in a gambling house by Ah Fi and Aw We and has gone to court.

A forest fire rages between Grass Valley and Nevada City. Three fires burn near San Juan.

Jewish business houses will close for religious observation.

The treason trial of Captain Dreyfus in France ended in a conviction and a pardon. Most of the world considers his conviction a brutal act of injustice.

Most of the mines will be giving their employees time off to take in the Admission Day picnic Saturday.

The tunnel at the Live Yankee Mine near Granitville is now 1650 feet long but pay gravel is still scarce.

William Jennings Bryan is on the presidential stump in San Francisco.

Samuel Bishop and Henry Hawk were blasted to smithereens in an explosion in the Mayflower Mine on Canada Hill. Their remains were gathered up in a fuse box.

Membership in the Grand Army of the Republic stands at 287,000, down from their height of 409,000 in 1890.

A new engine house is under construction at the N.C.N.G.R.R. depot.

A man named Callahan shot Nick Faryer in the thigh over a mining claim dispute near Sierra City.

England has 20,000 troops prepared to fight the Boers in Africa.

Nevada City will receive an up-to-date post office.

A daring train holdup in Arizona netted the bandits $10,000.

Jerry Goodwin, the U-Bet mining man, is recovering from a stroke.

Louie Tuck was killed by a falling tree near the Towle sawmill.

Two suspicious fires in Nevada City last night seem to have been set with the intention of torching the town.

There are complaints of young boys being too reckless with slung-shots on the city streets.

The cruiser Charleston bombarded forts in Subic Bay.

James Martin lost a fingernail when his hand was injured by an ore cart in the Massachusetts Mine.

An officer found a miner drunk on the streets. After dragging him off to the bastille, $60 was found on him. Lucky the law found him before a footpad did.

C. A. Arnold, 45, a cooper by trade, killed himself with a Colt .44 in Truckee.

A nugget worth $190 was brought over from a gravel claim on Shady Creek.

Yaqui Indians in Mexico had a battle with Mexican cowboys and drove them off, killing one man.

At noon, Sheriff Getchell will sell the Union Hotel for $8,000 on behalf of the Citizen's bank.

After visiting a house in the Tenderloin, some drunken young men started tearing up fences near a resort known as the Klondike. Officer Peterson chased them off, sending a pistol shot after them to speed them on their way.

John Moon, who lives on High Street, beat and kicked his wife who is in a `delicate' condition. He was brought before Judge Holbrook. What he should get is a good tar-and-feathering, or be tied to a hitching post and lashed.

A U.S. gunboat has been captured by the Insurgents and five men killed.

Rumor has it that Nevada City will soon have a female barber.

Several businesses have complained of shop lifters.

Some ladies have threatened to wear bloomers in town if something isn't done about all the expectorations left on the sidewalks that soil their skirts.

Charles Hoskin of Grass Valley died yesterday from a blow delivered by James Pendergast during a prizefight. It's likely prizefighting will be outlawed here.

Admiral Dewey returned to New York in triumph.

John Spaulding, superintendent of the South Yuba Water Company, contemplates a number of dams along the river.

A miner saw a young man on the street and thinking him an enemy, pummeled him severely before realizing he had the wrong man. Both appeared before the judge, one to express his sorrow, the other to reject pressing charges.

BOSS: Why do you want me to extend your vacation?

WORKER: It took me two weeks to learn to relax. It'll take me two more weeks to get used to working again.

Dr. McMurtry in later years

THE DEADLY DOCTOR

by

Brad Prowse

Forget The OK Corral
Or The Hickok-Tutt Duel
Even Bat Masterson and Sergeant King
This Was The Greatest Gunfight In The West

Dr. William McMurtry stood alone. His brother, brutally shot down, lay dying at his feet. A friend, Richard Kimball, was crumpled on the ground not far away, seriously wounded by the blast from a shotgun. Arrayed against Dr. McMurtry were a dozen armed men who had come there looking for trouble and spoiling for a fight. And then, one against twelve, Dr. McMurtry raised his pistol. Thus began what is perhaps the greatest gunfight of the Old West.

Dr. William McMurtry was both an unusual man and one typical of his time. Unusual in that he uprooted himself to trek for five months across what was then a forbidding and largely uncharted wilderness to California—twice. Typical because at that advent in our country's history, so many other men and women were brave and adventurous enough to dare to make such a grueling journey.

William McMurtry was born on August 15, 1802 in Harrodsburg, Kentucky. The family's progenitor—Joseph McMurtry—immigrated to the Colonies from Wales and settled in Philadelphia in 1734. In 1778 Joseph, along with his son John—William's father—followed Daniel Boone in crossing the Alleghenies into Kentucky, settling near Lexington. When the War of 1812 came along, young William McMurtry, ten, wanted to join as a drummer boy. He had to change his plans when his father, who manufactured bullets for the military, died.

McMurtry attended local Kentucky schools, then decided to pursue the profession of medicine. He did so by studying under an established doctor—a common practice at the time—in this case Dr. Tomlinson, a well known physician of that day. By the time McMurtry was twenty he had his own practice and within a few years had made a considerable fortune.

However, McMurtry had a love for the soil and for working with animals and he gave up his practice to buy a ten acre farm near

Elizabethtown, Kentucky. He built a saw mill and a race track and started breeding blooded horses. But the venture failed and McMurtry returned to medicine, hanging out his shingle near Louisville. In 1830 he married Sarah Van Anglen with whom he had five children.

McMurtry contracted malaria during this time and his health was poor...and his practice was suffering, too. He was living near Big Springs by now and many townspeople were poor and unable to pay him. So, when word of the California gold strike came with the 'news' that a man could "...pick up gold nuggets right off the ground...," McMurtry was led to cut loose from his roots and trade the fever of malaria for 'gold fever.'

On March 20th, 1849, along with his eldest son, John, eighteen, McMurtry left his home in Big Springs, Kentucky and traveled to St. Joseph, Missouri where he bought a covered wagon and four yoke of oxen. The two then crossed the wide Missouri. The records don't state if they traveled alone or with a wagon train but it might be supposed they would have joined with a train if one was leaving at the same time they were.

Covering around 15 miles a day, they followed the Platte River to Fort Laramie, then went on to Fort Bridger and thence across Utah and Nevada. They reached Honey Lake in the Sierras and followed a nearby fork of the Feather River to Oroville, California. The trip had taken them five months.

McMurtry and his son did some mining but were more successful as entrepreneurs, buying worn-out cattle from more recent emigrants for $30, fattening them and then selling them for $90.

By 1851, McMurtry had made enough money to invest in a restaurant in Grass Valley.

Grass Valley—and its sister town, Nevada City, three miles away—comprised the heart of an area called the Northern Mines. The two towns are located in the Sierra foothills, about sixty miles north-east of Sacramento. Though not as well known as the much-written about Mother Lode country to the south—towns such as Sonora, Columbia and Hangtown—the Northern Mines were much richer and didn't shut down until 1956. And that had nothing to do with a lack of gold! A labor dispute—and the low price of gold—caused the mine owners to toss in their hands and shut down operations.

With his hotel and restaurant, McMurtry now felt he was prosperous enough to make California his permanent home. At the end of 1851, leaving his son in Grass Valley, McMurtry caught a ship out of San Francisco and sailed for the east to gather up his family.

In March of 1852, McMurtry—and his wife and several other relatives—left Big Springs on his second sojourn across the plains to California. This time it took almost seven months to reach Grass Valley.

They also had several encounters with Indians—close enough to make them quite edgy—but none lead to any real trouble. McMurtry family history records that there were eleven in the party but whether that was the whole group that crossed the plains together or just the McMurtry outfit coupled to a larger train isn't known.

Once back in California, McMurtry continued to run his restaurant and hotel and started to farm some land down in the valley, not far from Chico, California. While he proved not to be a very good businessman at running the hotel, his farming operations did well. Over the years he would add to his holdings until `Butte Sylvania,' his ranch, included nearly three thousand acres of land on which he raised sheep, hogs, chickens and wheat. In the earliest days, Indians with flails threshed the wheat. Later, giant farm machines were used.

Sometime in the 1850s, McMurtry's brother, James McMurtry, who had apparently arrived in California in the intervening years, became part owner of a gold claim—the Larimer claim—on Osborne Hill, a mile or so east of Grass Valley. The gold property, probably located a few hundred yards to the south of present-day Highway 174, was one of many staked out on that promontory. The Larimer claim bumped up against one owned—at least in part—by Alexander Griffin, a butcher by trade.

Griffin's claim had started to yield gold and the vein lead right into the Larimer & Co. claim. Griffin stated that he would follow the lead and work it, even if it did go into the Larimer claim.

The Larimer owners tried to reason with Griffin, showing him the boundaries, but to no avail. Feeling the best defense was to start working the Larimer claim themselves, the Larimer people began to sink a shaft on their land. But Griffin had their work filled in and when a second shaft was started, Griffin swore he would fill that one, too, and take possession of the claim by force. To bolster his threat, on July 1st, 1858, Griffin armed—and supposedly fortified with liquor—a dozen men and proceeded to the two claims.

Hearing of Griffin's plans, James McMurtry, along with his brother and another partner in the property, Richard Kimball, went to Osborne Hill, hoping to protect the claim, if possible. The action drew a number of spectators and both sides began to talk. It was agreed to settle the problem peacefully by arbitration on the next day—Friday—and most of the onlookers left while Griffin and his men moved off a ways.

While the McMurtry's and Kimball stood there, the Griffin party, with Griffin himself riding about on horseback, returned, some stationing themselves near trees or logs. Griffin demanded that the new shaft be filled in. Nervous about the large number of opponents and their obvious belligerence, the three men, at Dr. McMurtry's insistence, started to move off, realizing the odds against them were too high.

Suddenly, a shot was fired by the Griffin party, followed by a volley of shots. James McMurtry, fell, mortally wounded, a bullet hitting him below the armpit and passing through his chest. Kimball also went down to the blast from a shotgun and was clearly out of the fight.

McMurtry now stood alone, facing a dozen armed men—perhaps more. He himself was only armed with a Colt revolver, which he had difficulty getting into operation as the pistol hung up on his coat as he drew it. But once clear of his clothing, he began to fire.

According to the news accounts of the fight, McMurtry fired in rapid succession. His pistol bucked in his hand and a man named Holland fell, dead. He fired again and a man named Carney slumped to the ground, dying. McMurtry moved, trying to dodge the bullets coming his way. His pistol roared once more and a third man, known as 'Coyote Jack,' was hit and would later die from the wound.

McMurtry continued to move around, dodging lead, as he kept firing, quickly but with accuracy. A fourth bullet from his Colt found Patrick Casey, then a fifth man and a sixth was hit. McMurtry's revolver was now empty and he bent down for his brother's pistol...but it wasn't needed. Unnerved by the quick-shooting doctor, the Griffin party now bolted, leaving the field to McMurtry and his dead brother and injured friend. The Battle of Osborne Hill was over. Griffin, according to newspaper accounts, had fled the scene at the outset of the shooting.

There are numerous accounts of the battle—both contemporary and later—and though generally agreeing, there are a few differences between them. In one, a sworn disposition taken for the trial of James McMurtry's killers, a member of the Griffin party said that the McMurtry side fired first—somewhat unlikely considering the odds.

Several accounts report that McMurtry's pistols was a 'small five-shooter,' which would make it a .31 Colt model 1849 pocket revolver. If every shot the good medico made went true, as is stated in all reports of the fight, it would mean five men of the Griffin party were hit. This may be correct as two accounts state that seven men were hit and that includes the dead James McMurtry and the wounded Kimball.

That McMurtry could do such deadly work with a little .31 Colt pocket model points up to both the nerve and skill of the man. On the other hand, at least one report of the fight says that the gun was a 'six-shot' which still could mean it was a model 1849, as they were made in that configuration too, or a larger 1851 Navy. It's unlikely he was carrying one of the larger dragoons. One thing all accounts agree on—each pistol ball sent forward by McMurtry found a home.

One newspaper article said there were between ten and fifteen men in the Griffin group while another says twelve to twenty. A third claims twelve and still another put their ranks at ten—all from contemporary sources! Twelve seems to be the operative number. It's also stated in two accounts that the weapon McMurtry retrieved from his brother's side was a derringer—in another account it is a revolver.

Six members of the Griffin crowd were tried and five—including Griffin—were sent to prison, sentenced to long terms. As all too often happens in our own time, the men were pardoned and set free within a few years.

The claims, over which so much blood was spilled, never amounted to much, though the mighty Empire Mine, situated at the foot of Osborne Hill, would turn out to be one of the Gold Country's most productive. No longer worked as a mine, today it has become a State park with many mining exhibits—but it still contains a wealth of gold.

McMurtry apparently gave up his Grass Valley interests soon after his brother's death. He settled in at his valley farm and started up his medical practice again. More than once he was known to saddle his horse in the middle of the night and, with medicine and instruments in his saddle bags, race to the side of a sick neighbor. He was active in the church and both he and his wife were known for their generosity and philanthropy.

Dr. William McMurtry died in Oakland, California on March 6, 1892, aged ninety-one years. There is nothing in the records to show that his life after the fight on Osborne Hill was anything but peaceful. But no one ever needed to question his nerve for there was that one day when he stood alone—his brother dead at his feet—facing a dozen claim jumpers with nothing but his revolver…and his courage.

100 YEARS AGO IN NEVADA COUNTY

December, 1899

by

Brad Prowse

The Coe mine will get a twenty-stamp mill.

Electricity will soon light the depot.

Six year-old William Enright of U-Bet died of scarlet fever and diphtheria. In Dutch flat, fifteen children died of scarlet fever in once week. No one is allowed in or out of that town.

December started out clear but rain—and snow—fell off and on until the end.

A water main tap on Prospect Hill blew out, wetting several houses.

Grass Valley is now a sewered city. Every lot has access to a hookup.

The Boer War is good for American business—175,000 pounds of canned beef and 1000 mules were shipped off to the British Army.

With the weather closing down the sawmills, Granitville is quiet.

Messrs. Luke and Temby have bought the Diamond Candy Factory.

General Lawton, an Indian and Civil War veteran, was killed in a cavalry charge in the Philippines. This leaves General Joe Wheeler, a Confederate Army veteran, as the only cavalry leader there.

James Maden of French Corral was robbed in broad daylight.

Considerable attention on the streets last night caused by a lighted paper balloon sailing through the air.

The Order of Redmen will hold a memorial marking 100 years since the passing of George Washington.

Two small boys, playing in the Manzanita Diggins east of the city, disturbed a Chinese man working a rocker. For some strange reason he chased them into town. Bystanders restrained the man.

Many of the Washington mines are working at full capacity. A. Pugh is running the Giant King day and night.

A tong war has broken out in Marysville's China Town.

Charles 'Pitchy' Baldwin was seriously maimed while toying with an 'unloaded' shotgun. Pitchy is not in his right mind. A year ago he slashed himself in a delicate region of the body and then sewed himself up with a common needle.

Target practice for Company `C' Sunday afternoon. At least 80% of the members must attend.

A coal famine threatens Grass Valley as the Southern Pacific seems reluctant to transport same over their tracks.

Ha Guey, the Chinese merchant, left for China. He may return next year.

Word from the Philippines is that Aguinaldo is ready to surrender.

John Buzza appeared before the grand jury on a bigamy charge—he has a wife in England as well as one here.

A horse is being raffled off for the benefit of the Catholic church in Cherokee.

Scores of girls jumped from a burning building in Reading, Pennsylvania when the Horst Hosiery Company caught fire. One woman dead, many injured.

Don't forget Donation Day on the 22nd!

The British lost hundreds in a fight with the Boers.

The Downieville stage was late yesterday. Many coaches up-country are on sled runners.

The Grand Jury report was a scorcher! They berated the Supervisors proposing to build a jail without a public vote and took Sheriff Getchell to task for the careless way he conducts his office.

Yaqui Indians battled over 4000 Mexican Troops near Rio Chico.

Wearing burnt cork, forty-odd ladies appeared as minstrels at the theater last night, featuring many new jokes and a lively cakewalk contest.

George White had telephone number 601 installed in his Lost Hill home.

Schools will close for the holidays.

The Army has ceased trials of the new wireless telegraphy citing financial differences with Mr. Marconi as part of the problem.

J. J. Schmidt was struck by a belt slipping off a pulley at the Cadmus mine.

A prisoner trying to light the old jail stove filled the place with smoke. Hoses and extinguishers were brought in but not needed.

The Philpot-Griffin feud in Kentucky has claimed two more lives.

Anti-debris spies say illegal hydraulicing has been going on at Moore's Hill and Relief Flat.

Turkeys are not so plentiful this year. Locally, they sell for 19 cents a pound.

A Nevada City married man went to the authorities and asked to be locked up as he was a on the verge of insanity and a danger to his family. He was released the next day, seemingly rational.

The roads around Blue Tent are so bad that horses sink into the mud and need to be pulled out.

In Nebraska, Jess Deane and Henry Spillman got into an argument, drew their six-shooters and blasted away. Deane was killed.

The UNION wishes a Merry Christmas to one and all.

The town rang with Christmas cheer the other night.

There are two ex-presidents now living—Harrison and Cleveland.

The Supervisors halted the tradition of serving prisoners a turkey dinner on Christmas. When the regular fare was presented, the prisoners pelted the jailers with it, going to bed hungry. Perhaps the sheriff should take them to the swellest hotel for a nice champagne dinner.

James O'Conner, born in Lake City, was killed in a cave-in at a mine near Chico.

Ben Wiley was arrested for allowing his horse to stand on the street for several hours.

"Heavens!" said a man. "What happened to your eye?"

"It's a berth mark," said the other. "I got into the wrong berth on the train."

ONE AGAINST THREE

by

Brad Prowse

Some men are lucky. Some are foolish. Some just have more nerve than the rest of us. And for Steve Venard to crawl his way up a rock-strewn ravine, alone, with three armed stage robbers somewhere just ahead of him, meant he was either foolish, lucky or brave...or maybe he figured, with Henry in his arms, that the odds were in his favor.

Nevada City still sits like a little slice of the 19th century Gold Rush in the tree covered slopes of California's Sierra foothills, about 60 miles northeast of Sacramento. With a population of around 3000 and the seat of Nevada County, the town has been preserved to look as much as possible as it did in the last century when its size wasn't that much different than it is now.

About 15 miles from Nevada City sits another former mining town, North San Juan. Time hasn't been as kind to North San Juan. Its single main street still holds a few business with brick facades...a real estate office, a long, narrow lunch counter run by an ex-Marine and his Oriental wife, one garage, a rough, gloomy bar that occasionally hosts small congregations of bikers of the type that the fastidious American Motorcycle Association wouldn't claim with a ten-foot membership card.

But, mostly, it's a place for the county locals to pick up their mail, a few gallons of high-priced gas and a six-pack. It's not the bustling mining town it was 100 years ago when regular Wells-Fargo shipments of gold went through to the banks in San Francisco.

The old road that once was the main connection between North San Juan and Nevada City is much the same as it was then, rutted and sparse, at least to the Edward's Crossing bridge. Once past the bridge, a narrow iron structure over the South Yuba, which runs quickly along here and into quieter pools downstream, the road begins a hard climb as it slithers around numerous curves, heading for Nevada City.

It was near here somewhere, on a flat stretch where the horses could blow a bit, that two stage robbers and their leader, George Shanks, stepped out of the brush and called it to a halt on May 16, 1866...and Steven Venard stepped out into local Gold Rush history.

California's mining territory, stretching up and down the length of the state for hundreds of miles, was probably inflicted with that traditional western bandit, the stagecoach robber, longer that any other area west of the Mississippi. One reason for this was the early jump California had on most western states because of the rush of `49.

While inhabitants of other, interior, territories were still dodging arrows and depending on scraggly-bearded mountain men to help them get around, California had a fairly sophisticated civilization going, even if people in the effete East might disagree...and still do today for that matter. Further, the California mining country was, and still is, a fairly rugged, sparsely settled area, fine for relieving people of gold and hiding it, if you were inclined toward banditry, but tough on keeping it if you were an express company.

Also, the Mother Lode and, to the north, the Northern Mines section of the state, used stagecoaches right up until the end of World War One, and kept the mines going well into the middle of the 20th century, long after many other frontier regions had run low on the precious metal. So road agentry seemed an attractive and easily plied trade in the California mountains. One stalwart who thought so, at any rate, was George Shanks.

Shanks appeared in California fairly soon after the Rush started. He may have been working in Coyote Diggin's, near Nevada City, as early as 1851. Later he drove a stagecoach for a short time and then drifted into doing odd jobs. He started using the alias of Bill Smith, lots of Smiths about in those days, and at one point tried to kill a former employer.

Peeved over a dispute about his wages, Labor opened up on Management with a pistol. Shanks fired, and missed, through the employer's window. During the Civil War Shanks joined the Union Army but was soon discharged, proving to be more trouble to the Federals than the Confederates were. He continued to get in and out of minor scrapes, making a general nuisance of himself.

But Shanks became more that just a pest when he started holding up travelers between the twin gold towns of Nevada City and Grass Valley. Grass Valley, along with Nevada City, formed the heart of the Northern Mines District, and sits three miles to the south-west of Nevada City. Shanks, fickle with his aliases, had now taken the name of Jack Williams, a bandit who had been hanged in Grass Valley in 1856. As the `ghost' of Jack Williams, he became a menace to any passerby between the two towns who might be carrying valuables.

For this new endeavor, Shanks took on two accomplices. One was Bob Finn, a deserter from a California regiment of volunteers raised during the war, and George Moore, a moody former convict who carried a picture of a woman and two children. When in his cups he would often take this picture from his pocket and gaze on it morosely.

So, on May 15th, the stage from North San Juan was rattling to the top of a long grade south of Edward's Crossing. It'd been dark when the stage left North San Juan to make an early connect in Nevada City, now about eight miles further on, for Sacramento. At 4:30 in the morning, the dawn just beginning to illuminate the tall pines lining the road, Shanks and his two companions stepped from the underbrush.

An invitation to descend, delivered under the muzzles of three revolvers, was quickly accepted by the six passengers and the driver. The team was unhitched and led about a hundred yards down the road. Then the Wells-Fargo strongbox was thrown down and while one man worked on it with a sledge, the other two outlaws entertained their prisoners, calling some of them by name.

The box wouldn't yield so a quantity of black powder was placed in the lock hole and touched off. No dice, so a second charge was laid and this time tamped in with mud and leaves. This did the trick and the top flew up at the slam of the charge and Shanks & Co. were $7,900 richer in coin and bullion.

While the bandits disappeared into the underbrush, the relieved passengers helped the driver hitch up the team. It was about 6 AM when they all rumbled into Nevada City and sounded the alarm. Sheriff Robert Gentry rounded up a posse of four men, one of whom was Steven Venard...and Venard brought Henry.

Venard was in his early forties. He'd come to California from his native Ohio. After trying a little mining he worked at freighting and as a storekeeper, even turning his hand to serving as a Nevada City marshall in 1864. He was noted for his quite demeanor...and his skill with the sixteen shot brass-framed Henry rifle he carried.

The Henry was a comparative newcomer on a scene where most firearms were still loaded with loose powder and ball, or at best, a paper wrapped version of same. The forerunner of the famous Winchester, manufactured by shirt tycoon cum arms maker, Oliver Winchester, it had been introduced in 1860 as the Henry, named after Winchester's chief designer, B. Tyler Henry. To this day, Winchester .22 cartridges carry a diminutive 'H' stamped on their base as a tribute to this man.

In 1866 the rifle would start bearing the Winchester name along with a side loading port and it was the direct ancestor of the famed 'Winchester '73.' The Henry differed from the latter mainly in that it had a brass frame instead of iron, it loaded from the front, much like a modern tubular-feed .22 rifle, and it used the .44 Henry rimfire. That cartridge, by the way, was about as powerful as a modern day .38 special, light for a rifle even then, and not as potent as the later .44-40 used in the `73. A few Henrys had been issued to troops during the war, but in 1866 they were still a rarity; a rifle capable of delivering sixteen aimed shots in about the same time a skilled man could load a conventional muzzleloader twice.

Sheriff Gentry and his posse, including Venard, rode out to the holdup site and scoured the surrounding area, mostly given to manzanita brush and some pines. The hardpacked ground didn't yield up many clues. It was decided that the bandits had probably headed towards Hoyt's Crossing, some two miles down river. The sheriff and two of the posse took off, heading by way of the road for Hoyt's Crossing, while Venard and another posse member rode their horses down towards Edward's Crossing, looking for tracks. The two men ran across footprints that soon left the road, going off to the left and paralleling the river below.

The terrain soon became too rough for the horses but is seemed apparent that the robbers were indeed heading toward Hoyt's Crossing. Venard told the man with him to take the animals back and try to catch up with the sheriff while he stayed on the trail, pressing along behind the bandits.

The land along this part of the Yuba is steep and full of ravines, some with water running in them. Most of the foliage is scrub brush and trees, generally pine with a little Douglas fir and madrone. A man working along here, trying to watch for footprints, carry a rifle and keep an eye out for armed and dangerous men would find it pretty rough going. Three men hauling the contents of a strongbox probably would not be moving too fast either.

Venard finally came to a place where the trail didn't continue downstream but instead, swung up a narrow steep ravine, Meyers Ravine, out of which flowed a swiftly running stream. Venard started up the rugged, boulder-strewn cut, picking his way over logs and brush. He went both unheard and unhearing, the cascading waters from a late spring runoff masking any other sounds.

The trail led up to a huge boulder sitting in the middle of the stream, looming up twenty feet above Venard. Brush, trees and smaller boulders at its base made it a natural island as the stream raced around either side of it. Not far from the base of this island was a precipice over which the water plunged fifteen feet. A fallen log spanned the distance from the bank at the top of the falls to the island.

Venard carefully walked over this rude bridge and stepped onto the island. Flanking the main boulder were two smaller rocks, forming an alleyway to the bigger stone's base that wasn't discernible until one was across the log bridge and onto the island. And there sat Jack Williams' 'ghost,' George Shanks, along with Bob Finn. Both men, spotted Venard at the same time he did them and they went for the pistols at their sides.

This was not an instance when a man had a lot of time to reflect on his choices in life. It was act by instinct or wind up wearing a marble headpiece in the local cemetery. Venard acted. The Henry came up and roared and twenty-five feet away, Shanks went down, shot through the heart.

Bob Finn, the second man, had rolled to the cover of a large boulder, his pistol cocked, the tip of his head showing now and again as he tried to get a shot off at Venard, still standing out in the open and probably wondering where the third man was. Venard was in a bind! He couldn't advance as it would only make him a better target for Finn's revolver. But to retreat across the log with an enemy behind him was equally impossible since it would put him in even greater jeopardy. And there was still that third man lurking about somewhere, unseen.

So Venard stood there, a fresh shell jacked into the Henry's chamber, waiting for what seemed like an eternity. First a tuft of hair, then a patch of skin, appeared over the top of the rock. Suddenly Finn popped up for a snap-shot and the Henry bellowed again. Finn fell dead, shot just below the eye.

Venard quickly gathered the sidearms, Finn's revolver still cocked, and made a search for the gold. He found it nearby, apparently intact. He hid the guns and gold under some leaves and then waded across the creek to get to higher ground. There was still Moore, hidden somewhere in the brush. As Venard splashed ashore, a man darted out of the brush about sixty yards ahead and started up the slope of the ravine. It was Moore.

Venard raised the rifle and fired, the report echoing up and down the narrow canyon. Moore fell, hit in the arm, but he jumped up again, a cocked pistol in his hand. He continued to scramble up the hill, keeping low, making as little a target for Venard's Henry as he could. He stopped, turned and tried to get a shot off. Venard fired again and Moore tumbled down the side of the ravine. He would not be taking the worn picture from his pocket to gaze at again. Moore was dead.

Venard returned to the road, exhausted from the rough climb and his fight with the bandits. He found Sheriff Gentry along with the Sheriff's brother, Lee, one of the possemen, riding along the road. They had heard the shots and, fearing the worst, had been searching for him. Venard told them he had found the gold and dispatched the outlaws. He seemed regretful he had to waste a second shot on Moore.

The road was soon swarming with a crowd of bandit seekers, brought there mainly by the one thousand dollars per head reward offered by Wells-

Fargo shortly after the Sheriff's posse left town. Many now went with Venard and the posse to view the scene of the battle and recover the gold.

By two o'clock the money box was safely in the hands of the Wells-Fargo agent in Nevada City. Less than ten hours had elapsed from the time of the robbery to the agents recovery of the strongbox contents. On checking the stolen money, it was found that a twenty dollar gold piece was missing. When Shanks' pockets were searched a twenty was found. It was promptly added to the haul which brought the amount recovered even with that stolen.

Steve Venard received the full $3000 reward from Wells-Fargo. Further, they presented him with a handsome new Henry rifle, engraved and mounted in silver and gold. Venard was also made a Lt. Colonel in the California State National Guard by Governor Low.

In the years that followed Venard and his Henry continued to be in demand. He was employed for a time riding shotgun on stage lines and later served as a payroll guard on the Central Pacific's pay train.

His last years, however, saw harder times. Steve Venard, aged 67, died on May 20th, 1891 in the county hospital near Nevada City. He was almost penniless and the hat had to be passed among those who had known him in order to gather enough to bury him in style.

Venard is gone. The stage bandits and the wild, free days of gold are vanished too. But the rugged hills endure, as does a wealth of gold, still buried but now beginning to stir men's thoughts again with new, cheaper ways to recover the shiny metal. The rocky creek where Venard had his fight continues to rush through the boulders and undergrowth, accessible to those tenacious enough to make the arduous two-hour jaunt to the site and back.

And Venard's presentation rifle can still be seen. Finally finding its way back to Wells-Fargo, it is today on view at the Wells-Fargo Bank History Room in San Francisco. It rests there, in its glass case, a proud tribute to the days when gold was there for the taking, either from the earth or the stage lines... as long as one was willing to risk the deadly aim of a man who could use a Henry rifle well enough to get it back.

100 YEARS AGO IN NEVADA COUNTY

February, 1900

by

Brad Prowse

Nevada City's night watchman Fowler was cited for neglect of duty and may be removed. He has allowed saloons to stay open after closing hours.

Stormy on the 3rd, than clear until storms mid-month and near the end.

Foley's is selling fancy naval oranges—25 cent per dozen.

The British and Boers continue to fight at Ladysmith.

Mrs. Jennie Fiske, 29, died this morning at the home of Mr. and Mrs. James Coley of Nevada City. She was to be married next month to Howard Marshall of Sacramento.

A new joss keeper has been elected in Nevada City's Chinatown. A large number of Chinese went over from Grass Valley and almost 1000 occidentals were also in attendance to take in the spectacle. In earlier days, when there were more Chinese here, the position of joss keeper was hotly contested.

Boers and British suffer heavily in fighting at Rensberg. Stories of British making captive Boers dig their own graves circulate.

John Tamblyn has opened a new horseshoeing shop on Broad Street in the old Clancy place—quality shoeing, $1.50.

Over 100 houses now stand in Floriston and the paper mill is expected to begin soon.

Hills Brothers coffee, 25 cents a pound at the Mitchell and Carson store.

James Buckett of Grass Valley has invented an adjustable bathtub seat and has applied for a patent.

The meeting of the American Association of Baseball Clubs in New York has proposed an organization consisting of a league of teams. Detroit Boston, Baltimore, Milwaukee, Chicago and St. Louis have signed up so far.

The famous old Banner quartz mine may be reopened.

Anna Combs, 15, of Hills Flat was stricken with severe hemorrhage of the nose. A doctor had to be called.

Marshall Deeble found two small boys, neither over ten years old, drunk on the street. They had been washing bottles in a Mill Street drug store and stole a bottle of whisky. One was sent home, the other spent a few hours in jail.

Ruth, a woman of the town, has left unceremoniously and with her went $65 belonging to a local young man.

Filipino insurgents captured a supply train and killed six American soldiers.

A Stereopticon lecture on a tour of England by Reverend B. D. Mayler will be held at the Congregational church Thursday.

A lad hit a mule led by a Chinese man on Broad street yesterday and the mule ran away.

The demented Japanese man brought to the jail the other day became violent and it took ten men to strap him down.

Pennsylvania Engine Company had a cotillion last night.

Company C will fall out Sunday at Hardscrabble rifle range for target practice.

Bill Cook, one of the most notorious desperados in Indian Territory, died in the penitentiary of consumption.

Smith, the boss candy maker, is producing bon-bons, caramels and other candies from pure Vermont maple sugar.

Carl and Fritz Meyer left this city over a year ago for the Klondike. They claim they can pan $500 worth of gold in a few hours.

Workers of the Sunset Telephone crew have lately imbibed too deeply of the flowing bowl after payday. One fell from a pole, another took a tumble from a buggy.

A terrible fire at Nevada City's Union Hotel, apparently started from a defective flue in the attic, resulted in a $20,000 loss.

In Arizona, an express car operator managed to drive off a band of robbers near Fairbanks with his Winchester rifle.

Two young boys named Trebilcox and Vincent were arrested for striking a Chinese laundryman with a rock, inflicting a deep gash. Both 11, they were let off with a lecture.

Stage driver Charles Secore was thrown from the box near Blue Tent when a stage wheel dropped into an especially deep pothole. Even the four horses had difficulty extricating the coach. Secore was badly bruised.

W.Y.O.D. Mine sued the Pennsylvania for $100,000, charging the latter ran workings into their claim.

Sailor Tom Sharkey knocked out Jim Jefferies in the second round of a ten rounder.

The young son of Frank Hall of Deer Creek is down with scarlet fever.

William Nichols, 12, of North Bloomfield, died of heart trouble.

Dewey claims that if the Nicaragua canal is built, American ships can protect it and fortifications are not needed.

Don't forget the Firemen's Ball tonight—purchase a ticket, even if you can't go.

Several wildcats have been killed in the Forest Springs area.

Constable Burt Alvord, of Wilcox, Arizona, has been implicated in a Southern Pacific train robbery.

Joseph Rodda, long time Grass Valley resident, hung himself. He suffered from melancholia.

Nevada and Pennsylvania Hose Companies received 500 feet of Victor jacket rubber hose.

By May of 1900 there will be about 100,000,000 Americans. There were fewer than 3,000,000 when Washington was president.

General Cronje and 4,000 men surrendered to British troops during the seige of Paardesburg.

COUNTRY CLEM (arriving at a big city hotel): "I suppose you ring a gong fer meals here."

HOTEL CLERK: "Oh there's no gong, sir. We serve breakfast from 6 to 11, lunch from 12 to 5 and dinner 6 to 11."

CLEM: "Jehoshaphat! When will I get a chance to see the city?"

The dapper bandit shortly after his capture

Nevada City was one of the mining towns Bart was familiar with

BLACK BART

The P.o. 8

by

Brad Prowse

Horses plunge and the stagecoach careens dangerously down the mountain road as Black Bart and his gang shoot it out with the guard in their attempt to rob strongbox and passengers.

Well, no. Maybe this happened in some old `B' movie or between the covers of a 1930s pulp western magazine. But the real Black Bart worked alone. And he never fired a shot in his 29-odd robberies. In fact, his shotgun was never loaded! Further, he only took from the Wells-Fargo box—he never bothered passengers. There may have been stagecoach robbers who were more successful in the size of their hauls, but there aren't many who had such a long and prolific run at helping to lighten Wells-Fargo's strongboxes.

Several mysteries have surrounded Black Bart—AKA Charles E. Bolton and Charles E. Boles—that have only in the last few years become better illuminated. One is of his earlier days, before he became a road agent. Another concerns the reasons for his grudge against Wells-Fargo. And how did Bart get around during his holdup sprees—spread out over eight years and hundreds of miles—and where did he stay? Lastly, what became of him in his later years?

Thanks to such recent books as `Black Bart, Boulevardier Bandit by George Hoeper—Word Dancer Press, and Black Bart, Elusive Highwayman-Poet by Laika Dajani, Sunflower University Press, today we can answer most of these questions.

The man who would become America's best known stagecoach bandit was born in Norfolk County, England in 1829. His family emigrated to the U.S. in 1830 or 1831 and settled in Alexandria, New York. Charles E. Bowles—the family name later became Boles—was one of ten children.

Boles received a `common' school education and worked on the family farm. It was noted he was quite athletic and a powerful walker—something that he would prove when, even though he was in his fifties, he became a stage robber.

125

Boles and a brother David went to California in 1849 and had some success in the gold fields. They went back east in 1852 but a few months later returned to the west coast, taking along another brother, Robert. Both David and Robert died of some illness soon after.

Boles again went east to farm near Decatur, Illinois. Sometime around 1856 he gained a wife, Mary Elizabeth Johnson. They had four children, Willie, Eva, Ida and Lillian. Boles volunteered for the Union Army in 1862, receiving a serious bullet wound and rising to the rank of lieutenant by war's end.

After the war, Boles returned to his family but soon left for the goldfields of Montana Territory. While he would write, he never returned home again.

In Montana, something significant to his later actions took place. Apparently Boles worked a claim that was served by a stream. Some other men tried to buy the claim and when Boles refused, they were able to cut off the water, rendering his claim useless. In letters home, Boles said that these men were in some way connected to Wells-Fargo. A daughter later related, "...he brooded on the, to him, extreme injustice of it till he took the step of getting it back in the way he did."

Boles last letters to his wife, at least until after his capture, were written in 1871. For all practical purposes, he had abandoned his family. He later claimed that his father was wealthy and would provide for them but it seems his wife subsisted by sewing clothes.

Between his leaving home, around 1867, when he was 40, until he began relieving stage coaches of their golden burden, Boles mined, drifted and perhaps worked as a school teacher. Whatever, on July 26, 1875, he held up his first stagecoach in Calaveras County, California. As Black Bart, Boles would be credited with making a total of 29 such unscheduled coach stops.

Bart's robberies were centered over California's northern half, mostly along the northern coast range, the Sierra foothills area and up toward the Oregon border. No two holdups were exactly alike, of course, but Bart pretty much followed a pattern. He worked alone, though on his first holdup he arranged sticks in the bushes to simulate the barrels of rifles held by a 'gang' that he 'talked' to during the robbery. He usually wore a white duster, a flour sack hood and carried a shotgun—one he later claimed was never loaded. He carried tools with which to break open the strongbox and he never bothered passengers. He did take the mail sacks though, which led the U.S. Government to add to the rewards Wells-Fargo offered.

Thomas B. Forse, the stage driver during Bart's 22nd robbery, June 14, 1882, said, "Bart always picked out a place where he could see. He had fieldglasses, too. All a driver could do was obey orders."

Bart didn't use a horse, traveling about on foot. This was interesting in that it pointed up to Charles Boles being in pretty good physical shape. Undoubtedly he was, on occasion, able to hitch rides with passing teamsters and private vehicles. Traffic was brisk in the gold-busy foothills and travelers would have been welcome for the company and possible news they provided. But shanks mare was Bart's favored method of moving about.

After his capture, many in the area of the holdups recognized Boles as Black Bart. It may seem strange that no one ever considered turning Boles in as a possible suspect. One reason may have been the natural reluctance to pry into the business of others in those days. Also, in his fifties, Boles may not have looked much like a bandit. Though he had limited formal schooling, he affected the demeanor of a gentleman and—when living in San Francisco between his forays into the foothills—pulled off the part of a refined, moderately successful mining man.

According to a Mr. Halping, whose sister ran a saloon frequented by Boles, Who he knew as Charles E. Bolton, "[He] was an educated man—he spoke seven languages. I used to talk German to him. He never got down to the business he was in but he was very talkative. He was a gentleman. Always well dressed, too. He was heavy-set, a man about five foot ten inches. An active man, too."

Another factor may have been that Wells-Fargo was not all that widely a loved institution. They pretty much had a shipping monopoly in the region and were sometimes felt to be using a heavy hand in maintaining their control—and hefty rates—in the area. Since Black Bart wasn't taking life, only strongboxes, his amusement value to the public gave him a measure of protection.

Bart struck twice in 1875, in Calaveras County and Yuba County. In 1876 he hit but once, in far northern Siskiyou County, and once in 1877 in Sonoma County, near the coast. It was at this site he left his first lines of doggerel:

> I've labored long and hard for bread
> For honor and for riches,
> But on my corns too long you've tread
> You fine haired Sons of Bitches.
> Black Bart, the P o 8.

The last line of rhyme was often changed to `You folks in fancy britches' for newspaper consumption.

On July 5th, 1878, his next strike, Bart left another `poem.'

> Here I lay me down to sleep,
> To wait the coming morrow.
> Perhaps success, perhaps defeat,
> And everlasting sorrow.
> Let come what will, I'll try it on,
> My condition can't be worse;
> And if there's money in that box
> Tis munny (sic) in my purse.
> Black Bart, the P o 8.

This would be Bart's second and last missive to Wells-Fargo but it was enough to really capture the public's imagination and put Black Bart on the front page.

There were three holdups in 1878, three in 1879 and five each in 1880, 1881 and 1882.

While probably the most prolific of California's stage robbers, Bart's haul from these robberies may not have been all that great. Some hauls were in the thousands of dollars, others netted him less—one strongbox held 35 cents!. It has been said he may have gotten as much, overall, from the mail sacks as the strongboxes. An estimate of around $10,000 to $15,000 as a total haul is probably a pretty fair estimate but it might have been more. Wells-Fargo didn't always disclose their strongbox losses. It may have been those `undisclosed' losses were pretty hefty. Of course, in a day when a man could live pretty well on $50 a month, even $15,000 wasn't to be laughed at.

James B. Hume was Wells-Fargo's Chief of Detectives and he wasn't even smiling. Within weeks of Bart's first holdup, Hume had reward posters—promising $250 and a share of any recovered loot—for the capture of the bandit who would not be known as Black Bart until the first poem showed up.

Most of Bart's robberies were fairly routine. Occasionally he operated at night. And after Wells-Fargo got smart and started bolting the strongbox to the coach, getting at the loot became more risky for Bart.

Bart's tenth robbery was a stage coming out of Bass Station, near Redding, California, October, 25, 1879. Driver Jimmy Smithson said, "It was a bright moonlight night and I was coming around the point and (Bart) was in the grass there. As I came around, my leaders jumped as though they were going over one side. There was someone ahead. 'Hold up your hands,' he said. 'Throw out the box!'"

"I said I can't do it; it's chained down."

Bart ended up using an axe to smash in the box enough to extract the treasure.

On November 20, 1880, Bart made a another nighttime holdup near the California-Oregon border. While trying to get the bolted-down strongbox out, the driver, brandishing an axe, managed to chase Bolton off with only a mail sack as his trophy for a night's work.

On July 13, 1882, five miles west of LaPorte on the LaPorte-Oroville run, a Wells-Fargo guard managed to crease Bart's scalp with a rifle shot, a scar he carried from then on. Bart got zip from that one.

For the most part, the earlier holdups were spaced far enough apart that Boles could have returned to San Francisco, his home base, between forays. But when located on a map, the 29 robberies show a clustering of locations and dates. The robberies of July 25, and 30, 1878, were physically close together as were those of October 2 and 3, 1878, the three in September of 1880, the two in October of 1881, two more in December of that year and three holdups in 1882. This indicates that Boles had places to hole up somewhere within hiking distance of these holdup sites when planning them. (Incidentally, on his last holdup, Boles hiked through over 80 miles of rough country in three days).

Boles, after his capture, said he often stayed with people living at remote ranches and cabins, providing gossip and conversation to people starved for word of the outside world. At the same time, he could check on stagecoach schedules, when gold shipments were likely, various escape routes and the like.

In 1962, Frank Reader, then in his nineties, gave an interview to a Nevada City journalist, Bob Paine. Frank told Paine how his father once owned a sawmill some miles out of Nevada City. One day a man who gave his name as Martin showed up. Reader's father gave him a job on the green chain and provided him with a cabin to live in. (The green chain is one of the most physically arduous jobs in a sawmill. That Boles, in his fifties, could fulfill that job is a testament to his physical condition).

One time, Frank reader recalled, his father didn't have enough money on hand to meet his sawmill payroll and said he would need to go to town for funds. 'Martin' then offered to loan Reader $300 to meet the payroll—this from a man earning $2.00 a day!

'Martin' was a reliable worker, though he occasionally had to leave for short periods of time. He even took a shine to little ten-year-old Frank. It wasn't until later that Reader's father realized that Martin's absences always proceeded a relatively local stage robbery.

Bart's depredation drove the Wells-Fargo detectives frantic! Their losses to the bandit weren't as galling as the amount of time they needed to spend chasing him down, time that could have been better spent on investigating train robberies, internal thefts and the like. Also, their inability to nail Bart was good fodder for the press. But, in fact, they had little to go on. There was no good description of Bart and in his guise as a mining man, he had no record, was not much of a drinker and, in fact, mixed in rather well with San Francisco society, even occasionally squiring widowed matrons to various social affairs.

However, like most criminals, if they push their luck too far, it will run out. It ran out for Boles/Black Bart on November 3, 1883 on the Sonora-Milton Road, in the same spot his first holdup had taken place.

The stage had stopped at the Reynolds Ferry Hotel before tackling the steep grade ahead. Nineteen-year old Jimmy Rolleri, whose mother owned the hotel, asked driver Reason McConnell if he could hitch a ride up the hill. He was carrying a rifle, intending to get a little game.

"Sure," McConnell said. "Glad to give you a ride." And Rolleri claimed aboard.

Halfway up the grade, young Rolleri got off the coach, intending to start hunting. The coach went on for another thirty minutes, nearing the ridge when a man in a hood jumped out, threatening with a shotgun and demanding the driver stop and throw down the box.

"I can't" McConnell said. "It's bolted to the floor of the stage."

McConnell stalled for time, saying the wheels needed to be blocked as his brakes were bad but, eventually, Black Bart chocked the wheels and then went to work on the strongbox.

Ordered to take the team up the road, McConnell noticed Rolleri moving uphill, out of sight of Bart but visible to McConnell. The two men joined up and moved back toward the coach, Mcconnell carrying the rifle, a .44 Henry.

Bart saw the two coming and, gathering his loot, took off running into the brush. McConnell fired twice to no effect when Rolleri asked to take a shot and, on this third shot, both men saw Bart stagger slightly, dropping some of the mail he'd plundered. But Bart, his left wrist grazed, recovered himself and was soon safely lost in the brush.

Boles ran for his life, later telling lawmen that "I was so overcome with surprise and fatigue that a ten-year old could have captured me."

It wasn't long after the authorizes were notified of the latest holdup when Detective Hume showed up, hot on the trail. Despite a loss of clues because of all the sightseers trampling about before Hume got there, enough was found to nail Bart, for among the items he left behind was a handkerchief, the laundry mark F.X.O.7 stenciled on it.

From there on it was just routine police work to track down the laundry mark, used by one of ninety-odd laundries in San Francisco. The F.X.O.7 coding designated laundry belonging to a Charles E. Boles—a respected and refined mining man.

When he was picked up, walking along the streets of San Francisco, he kept the pretense going, insisting he was a respectable mining man long after Hume and his detectives had gathered enough evidence to convict him. Finally, Boles broke down and confessed—to that one, last holdup, no more. He waived a trial, plead guilty and received six years in San Quentin prison.

Boles later owned up to the rest of the robberies and the fact he was Black Bart, a name he'd picked from a novel, The Case Of Summerfield, which had been printed some years earlier in the Sacramento Union.

Boles was released in January of 1888 after serving four-and-a-half years, getting time off for good behavior. The newspapers were there to record the event and a reporter for the San Francisco Chronicle asked if he would consider returning to his ways as a highwayman. Bart replied he was done with crime. Another reporter asked if he would write more poetry. Bart turned with a mock frown.

"Young man, didn't you just hear me say I would commit no more crimes?"

While he had started writing his wife again, he never returned to his family. Then, despite his being watched by Wells-Fargo agents, after staying around San Francisco for a month, Charles Boles—Black Bart— disappeared.

What happened to Boles after that has remained a mystery to this day. There were a few stage holdups shortly after that could have been pulled off by Black Bart. At first Detective Hume seemed to think they were, then later recanted.

There were reports of his living in Oakland, California, of being killed during a Nevada stagecoach holdup, of moving to Japan for the rest of his life. His wife, Mary Boles, listed herself in the 1892 Hannibal, Mo. directory as a 'widow,' but this may have been only a convenience.

At least one newspaper carried a short piece on Bart in late 1897, saying he had passed away back east and A New York newspaper printed an obit of a 'Charles E. Boles, a civil War veteran' in 1917. And he was 'spotted' by various people over the years here and there.

A further mystery was how did Bart finance all—or any—of these movements about the country and/or world? One version was that he tapped into some funds hidden away at the time of his arrest. Then there was the possibility he'd returned to stagecoach banditry. Still another—always denied by Wells-Fargo but upheld by many contemporaries—was that Wells pensioned him off at $125 a month—cheap insurance to keep him away from their shipments. But there may be another answer.

In late 1888 or early 1889, Frank Reader's sister found a visitor at her front door. She gasped as she recognized the man who had once been their employee, `Martin.' Please could he visit the cabin where he once stayed? Yes, said Hattie.

He was at and around the cabin for about an hour, then reappeared at the door. He thanked her and slipped a silver dollar into her hand. Then he walked away. No one ever saw Black Bart again.

END

FIVE PISTOLS

Against
ONE CHAIR

by

Brad Prowse

Being handy with a gun was a useful skill in our country's wilder days and not a few men worked to attain that expertice. Being good with a chair, however, was a somewhat rarer ability but at least one man was good enough with a chair to drive off five express-office bandits. Here's how.

Today Truckee, California, is not thought of as having been a `wild and woolly' town such as Tombstone or Dodge City. A passer-by on the nearby Interstate sees only a small but growing little town, nestled just below Donner Summit. But in the 1860s and 70s, it was, in the words of one writer, `...overrun with bad characters...(that) created a great deal of trouble..."

The town, founded in the early days of the Gold Rush, was relatively quiet until the coming of the continental railroad. After the Central Pacific established a major rail facility there the town became an important stopping point for the trains just finishing the hard climb over the Sierras or about to make the descent into the Sacramento Valley far below. The town also supplied winter-cut ice to the valley in the summer and had a extensive sawmill industry. Miners, railroad workers, lumberjacks and the usual gamblers, toughs and ladies of the evening—it was a lively place.

On the evening of April 22nd, 1869, a Thursday, H. K. `Hank' Brown was reposing in a large wooden chair in the back of his store—Burckhalter & Brown—reading a paper. April was still `winter' in mile-high Truckee and the warmth of the stove was welcomed. The store also acted as an agent for the a Union-Pacific Express and nearby his cashier, W.T. Loudon, was counting the day's receipts. Spread out on a tray was about $18,000—this when such a sum was more than a working man might make in his lifetime.

Suddenly, four masked men, their features hidden by sacks, rushed in through the front door. One pointed a revolver at Loudon's head, demanding the money. A second did the same kindly service for a Frank Pauson, a bysstander, as two more robbers came through the rear door, one of whom covered W.T. Nicholson, a salesman, who was standing behind the stove. Brown, meanwhile, continued to sit in his chair, feet still up on the counter.

At first, Brown thought it was a couple of local wags having some fun. "Boys, you lay yourselves liable to get badly hurt," he called out—and then went back to his reading.

One robber roughly grabbed his wrist, waving a pistol under his nose, and Brown jumped out of the chair, crying out, "By God damn, this means business!"

Before anyone could react to Brown's sudden animation, he swung the chair over his head and crashed it down—along with a lamp hanging from the ceiling—upon the head of the startled robber. The man got off a shot as he fell backwards, but it missed Brown. The man cocked his pistol for a second try but Brown swung the chair upwards, hitting the pistol and putting the shot into the ceiling.

The man guarding Nicholson also fired but Nicholson flattened himself out on the floor and was unhurt. Brown, meanwhile, continued to describe parabolic curves with the chair until both robbers were driven out the back door with sore heads, leaving Brown behind with a chair shattered to fragments.

The men in the front of the store, unnerved by Brown's actions, took off running. One, in his haste, discharged his pistol while running outside, putting the ball into his foot. No one managed to get away with any loot.

The injured bandit, John Morton Blair (in one account, John Moultrie) later died of the effects of the shot to his foot. Three of the others, Chris Blair, (possibly a brother of the injured man) Billy Forest and a man known as 'Lee,' eventually ended up in prison. (Though Forest and Blair beat the robbery rap, both were convicted of another, earlier, offense.)

And Brown? He lost no money. He was not injured. And one supposes he replaced the old chair he'd been sitting in at his stove for a new one—unless he decided to get a pair of chairs so that he could claim to be a 'two-chair' man!

END

"Tile Little Grave Today"

THE LITTLEST ARGONAUT

by

Brad Prowse

Travelers driving along the stretch of Highway 20 just east of Nevada City are often surprised when the long expanse of towering pines is suddenly relieved by the sight of a grave enclosed by a white picket fence. If they take the time to stop, they learn that this is the burial place of a small child. Guarded by two tall pines, the little grave of Julius Albert Apperson has lain silent and alone, except for passing cars, these past 140-odd years.

Julius Apperson's parents were among the earliest settlers in the area. They arrived around 1851, when the Gold Rush was still in its youth and Old Sacramento was new. The Appersons were married a short time later in Nevada City.

In 1858 the couple and their—by then—four children, moved into a house that the senior Apperson had built in the forest above Nevada City. One cool, May evening, shortly after moving to their new home, the children built a fire of wood chips near the house. All the children ran about, playing around the dancing flames, when suddenly Julius came too close and the left leg of his trousers caught fire.

Julius's mother tried to put out the flames in her own clothing and, failing this, dashed across the road and dropped the small boy into a watering trough. Julius's left leg and side were badly burned. After lingering a week, the boy died, aged two years, two months and twenty-five days old. He was buried by his grief stricken parents between two pine saplings not far from their home.

The Appersons later moved away and Martin Marsh, a resident of the area, took an interest in the grave, placing a wooden marker at the site in 1863. The marker was repainted several times over the years but it wasn't until 1948, when a woman from the San Francisco Bay Area—a Mrs. Gladys Sherman—ran across the grave, took an interest in it and had a picket fence placed about grave. For many years Mrs. Sherman continued to come up and keep the fence in repair.

In 1970 the grave site was declared a historical point of interest by Nevada County and the Grand Parlor, Native Sons of the Golden West, erected a large memorial on the spot.

Many people tend to think of the Forty-Niners only as the sturdy pioneer and his faithful wife, following their wagon westward. Others dote more on the miner, searching for gold, or the gambler, searching to relieve the miner of any gold he might find. We sometimes forget that many pioneers were small and helpless, argonauts who chased no dream of new land or easily won riches. They were in the vanguard of civilization through chance, not choice. Julius Albert Apperson, died May 6, 1858, the littlest argonaut, was one of these.

THE OLD SLAVE MINE

by

Brad Prowse

When the topic of slavery in America is brought up, it usually brings to mind a scene of African-Americans toiling away under a hot sun in the cotton fields on some Southern plantation. Few would come up with an image of these same black men and women working in California's Sierra foothills, digging gold along with the Argonauts of `49. But that's just what happened to the slaves owned by Colonel William F. English during those first, hectic years after the discovery of gold in California.

Col. English was a native of South Carolina, though he also had business dealings that took him to Georgia and Florida. Intrigued by the discovery of gold in California, English, acting as a representative for some wealthy Georgia planters, went there in 1851. In the Sierra foothills, about 50 miles north-east of Sacramento, he ran across a claim staked out by two men, Abel and Porter. It showed good color and English secured an interest in the claim and returned to the east.

A big problem with such a project was getting workers. White men brought out to work the mines often took off to find their own claims as soon as they arrived—even when they had agreed to stay long enough to work off their passage. Most would simply desert into the gold country. To English, a Southerner and slave holder, the solution seemed simple—use slaves to work the mine.

English sold his holdings in the East and selected a group of slaves to take to California. English and his party traveled to Philadelphia to outfit, meanwhile waiting to see if California was going to be admitted as a salve state or free. It has been reported that the slaves chosen to accompany English were anxious to go to California. Whether the fact that California would end up as a `free' state had anything to do with their attitude is not known.

After a trip around the Horn, English and his slaves—numbering as few as 66 or as many as 175, both numbers have been reported—along with mining machinery, finally reached San Francisco. Soon English and his company were located at the claim, named the Kentucky Ridge Mine, about five miles from Grass Valley and one mile from Rough & Ready, another booming village.

English was said to be a kind master. Once the land was cleared and space for operations set up, the slaves quickly became adept at mining. Rough cabins were built—perhaps as many as forty—and food was plentiful. Soon a semblance of family life was enjoyed by the slaves.

A vertical shaft was sunk and the slaves hauled the broken ore to a mill a quarter mile away. The tailings from the mine proved to be something of a disappointment but their placer operations, set up nearby, did better. While the men did the heavy work the women cooked, kept house and washed clothing for the company.

In late summer of 1852, Col. English mounted his horse and left for a trip to the town of Nevada City about six miles away. In his saddlebags was a considerable sum of gold. It would be his last ride.

English was found on the road between the mine and the town, dead from a shot from his own pistol. Just what happened is still disputed. According to Edmund Kinyon in his book, 'The Northern Mines,' "...English was found unhorsed and dead (from) a shot fired from his own pistol...whether by design, accident or highwayman..."

Kinyon, writing around the middle of this century, stressed the point that the Colonel was on his way to town and that his saddlebags were empty. This would point to a likely robbery and murder. However, there is a contemporary account in the Friday, September 3, 1852 edition of the Nevada Journal, published in Nevada City. (In its earliest incarnation, Nevada City was known simply as 'Nevada.' It became incorporated in 1856 as 'Nevada City') The Nevada Journal depicts the incident differently.

"He (English) was thrown from his horse while on his way from this city (Nevada) to Kentucky Flat. He had a small gun...the muzzle of which struck him in the breast and discharged..."

It seems from this contemporary account that English was heading BACK to his claim, probably AFTER he had left his gold in Nevada (City). Some speculated he may have committed suicide, as it was known the claim was not paying out as expected. Others held to the highwayman theory and still others called it—as the paper indicates—an accident. In any case, English was buried in the old Pioneer Cemetery in the town of Nevada.

The mine floundered and his wife freed the slaves—if indeed, they weren't already technically free by being in California. Some of the slave's surnames were Sanks, Mills, Thomas, Green, Allen, Owsley, Striker, Fair, Davis, Smith and Page.

In the East, relatives of English attempted to reclaim the slaves—or, lacking that, make them pay for their own freedom. Legend has it that some did so. Jordan Owsley paid $1000 for his wife, who had been left back in Georgia. But after sending the $1000, the ante was raised to $1200. Owsley decided to cut his losses and married a Creole woman. His money was eventually returned but the fate of the first Mrs. Owsley is not known.

Many of the former slaves settled in the area and made up the principal black population of Grass Valley for decades, even founding their own African Methodist Episcopal Church. They worked at jobs around town as laborers and domestics. A few were able to raise themselves above the ordinary. Frank Allen was a noted local fiddler and Willie Page, something of a musical prodigy, eventually opened a music store in Sacramento that became a mecca for enthusiasts of exotic music.

Caroline Allen, one of the slaves who came around the Horn, was about 50 years old in 1851 when she rode into Rough & Ready one day and stuck a cottonwood switch she'd been carrying into the ground. It was a wet season and the switch took root and became a large tree, standing until July, 1962, when it came crashing down. Allen herself died in the early 1900s.

(The Union, a Grass Valley newspaper, printed the following in January of 1898: "A colored man named Walker arrived on the train from Colfax, claiming he mined in Rough & Ready in 1848. He was surprised to see how the town has grown but was sad not to find his brother nor any of those he mined with 50 years ago." It's likely this man had been one of the slaves at the Kentucky Ridge Mine).

The mine—now known locally as the Old Slave Mine, was worked at from time to time over the years without really living up to its early promise. The shaft is still there, though largely overgrown and silted in. It bears silent witness to the strength, skill and effort made by men and women who came to dig for gold as slaves but stayed to find something more precious in the gold fields—their freedom.

March, 1900

by

Brad Prowse

The large new coach bought for the Narrow Gauge has been fitted with neat cane chairs and will become part of the regular passenger run.

The dance given by the young men of North San Juan was both a social and financial success. Merrymakers attended from the various ridge towns and tripped the light fantastic to the early hours.

Heavy storms—off and on—early in the month, then fair weather.

The old road to the Banner mine through Canada Hill is being reopened as the Banner, once a high producer, is hoped to be operating again within a year.

Boers defeated at Ladysmith by British troops.

Ralph White was arrested for receiving stolen goods from Lee Shoecraft—machinery stolen from local mills.

Dr. G. B. Carr shot a burglar who threatened him in his home. The man will live.

Charles Lansing has been passing bad checks in Truckee and is presently in jail.

Mr. and Mrs. Peter Martell of Rough & Ready have been married for fifty years.

Major J. S. McBride is dangerously ill at North San Juan from inflammation of the bowels.

Two Indians have been arrested near Chico for the murder of Billy Simpson. There is great excitement among Indians there and the prisoners are being closely guarded.

A dance will be given on the 17th at Sweetland school house for the benefit of the Catholic church in Birchville.

No new cases of smallpox in Truckee—the scare seems to be over.

And health officers removed the quarantine from the home of Frank Hall on Deer Creek. His two children have recovered from scarlet fever.

John Fisher, son of E. C. Fisher, of French Corral, died of gastric fever. He was 21.

A hobo was arrested for using foul language on the streets. He attempted to hit Marshall Deeble who threw the man to the ground and put the nippers on him.

A blasting hole with a slow fuse almost killed Patrick Brophy at the Delhi mine.

Jim Jefferies defeated Jack Johnson (colored) in a 20 round go in Philadelphia.

New regulation leggings were received by Company C the other day.

A runaway at the train station saw a horse and buggy driven by Frank Hall bolt away to Bank Street where it jumped a fence, landing in a yard several feet lower than the road, the buggy wheels caught up in the fence. It was a strange sight, the horse down in the yard and the wagon above him at street level.

Dr. C. W. Jones claimed he shot a 200 pound mad dog in his front yard.

Fred Odgers received smashed fingers at the Maryland mine when a section of timber fell on his hand.

In Washington, Peter Craft, 75 and a native of Sweden, having suffered from diseases for a long time, took his life with strychnine. He died quite painfully over several hours.

The report of Dr. Jones killing a mad dog was apparently just a joke played by the Doctor on a reporter.

Mr. S. C. Corbin, a prominent citizen of Auburn, is in town looking for his son Kay, 14, a runaway.

A group of boys attacked a Japanese man last night but were chased off by Night Watchman John Frank, who caught one of the lads. The boy said it all started with a keg of beer in the Lincoln schoolyard. Arrests are expected.

The 38th Infantry killed 24 Insurgents in an ambush in the Philippines.

William Stevens and Joseph Cunha had hot words over 25 cents the former was alleged to have withheld from the latter. After a lively fight, Marshall Deeble and Officer Frank placed Stevens under arrest and took him to Judge Green's court where he there made a break for liberty. Marshall Deeble quickly cooled his ardor for flight by a few raps on the head with the butt of his pistol. He was fined $30.

The Milton to Copperopolis stage was held up and $17 taken.

One man tried to kill another on Spring Street by firing five shots at him. All missed. They were Swedes or Italians, both worse the wear from drink.

City Trustees and the City Clerk mapped out seven new voting precincts for the town.

James Starr, 19, of Copperopolis, pleaded guilty of the stage delivery there.

Immigration officials in San Francisco and Seattle are alarmed by the large influx of Japanese. In the last week over 700 of the little brown men have set foot on these shores.

A sheriff's posse at Navajo Springs, New Mexico lost two men killed while taking five cattle rustler's captive. Two escaped.

CLASSIFIED AD:

The person who stole the feathers from our mother's hat is well known to us. If it is desired to avoid trouble, they will please return same immediately. SNELL BROS.

The Black Kentuckians appeared at the theater, presenting plantation songs, and good old fashion dark fun consisting of wing, buck and ragtime dancing, all ending with a cakewalk.

John McBean's fine home in Washington burned to the ground. A defective flue is suspected.

They say dead men tell no tales. Well, the living sure tell tales about them.

JIM WEBSTER

The Only Bullet That Could Kill Him

Was No Bullet At All!

by

Brad Prowse

Jim Webster's marksmanship with rifle and pistol was legendary, to such a degree, that, when he turned to outlawry, few men would dare to challenge him. At the command of `Hands up,' there were none so foolhardy as to go for their own weapons.

Jim Webster was, as far as the record shows, mining peacefully in the Timbuctoo area of California in the early 1850s. The town of Timbuctoo once lay a dozen miles into the Sierra foothills, above the valley town of Marysville.

In 1855, Webster had a dispute with claim jumpers over a claim. It ended up with Webster shooting all three of the men dead in a nearby ravine. These men became the first inhabitants in the newly established Timbuctoo cemetery.

Unwilling to wait for the blessing of the law for what he considered self-defense, Webster decided to take it on the lam. For the next two years Webster would be a terror in the area, pulling off a number of robberies. He often visited towns further up into the hills such as Nevada City and Washington, but none dared to step forward to take him on as it was generally known that Webster was not afraid to shoot—and he never had to shoot twice.

During 1856, in and around Nevada City, the county seat of Nevada County, Webster depredations were almost a nightly occurrence. Finally, he was captured and lodged in the local jail—only to soon escape with another prisoner. A week later, Nevada City Marshal Henry Plummer (yes, he of later Virgina City, Montana, fame!) and Bruce Garvey recaptured Webster near Smartsville. Webster and his men we're caught napping, literally, and had no chance to grab the pistols they had placed under their pillows. Webster was retuned to a cell.

Not to be daunted, Webster—this time along with two members of the equally notorious Tom Bell gang—broke jail again. The next day, it was learned by the authorities that horses and equipment were hidden in Gold Ravine, near Gold Flat, not far out of Nevada City and this news ended up bringing tragedy to the local law enforcement agencies. Somehow or other a great miscommunication took place as two different parties—each unknown to the other—went to the location, to await the outlaws.

It was nearly dark when the first group arrived, a party made up of local Gold Flat residences, led by L.W. Williams. A second group, a sheriff's posse, led by Sheriff W.W. Wright came on the scene shortly after. The Williams party had already concealed themselves when the Sheriff's men appeared upon the scene. William's men watched in anticipation as Plummer, in full view, but unrecognizable in the near-darkness, proceeded down the ravine.

Plummer whistled and several other posse members came into view and the Williams party was sure they had their escaped outlaws. The last of Plummer's men to appear noticed G.H. Armstrong, one of the Williams group, hiding behind a tree and alerted others of the Sheriff's posse of the fact. Sheriff Wright, his revolver at the ready, ran toward the man and someone—it was reputed to be Williams himself—thinking Wright was an outlaw, fired.

The battle was then on, becoming general, and over fifty shots were fired before Plummer recognized Williams' voice and saw his face in a pistol flash. Once the gunfire had died out and lanterns procured, Sheriff Wright was found dead, his jaw pieced by Williams' bullet and his body hit by forty balls from a shotgun fired by T.L. Bladwin.

Special Deputy David Johnson was also dying but managed to walk to Armstrong's house before he expired. Wright was the first of three Nevada County sheriff who would perish on the job by gunfire—all in the 1800s.

Webster was arrested again a few weeks after the death of Wright. He was picked up in Yuba County and placed in the Marysville jail. In February of 1857, he was convicted of grand larceny and robbery and sentenced to the penitentiary for 25 years. Two others of his gang, Lee Shell and Shelly received five and ten years respectively.

But Webster again exhibited his prowess at breaking jail by escaping in August of 1857, along with eight others. However, his luck was running out. While hiding in the Coast Range, he quarreled with a gang member and ordered him out of camp under pain of death. Unknown to Webster, the man hung around and after Webster fell asleep, the man drew the bullet from Webster's gun.

In the morning, Webster awoke to find the man sitting on a nearby stump, watching him. Webster exclaimed, "So you didn't go?" seized his rifle and fired the now-blank charge at the man. The man then coolly raised his own gun and shot Webster dead.

Thus was killed a man who was too good with a gun to be faced on even terms. In a few years, Jesse James, William Bonney and Wild Bill would all fall victim to the same set of circumstances.

END

100 YEARS AGO IN NEVADA COUNTY

June, 1900

by

Brad Prowse

The 'Last Days of Pompeii' was presented at Mt. Saint Mary's musical hall under the auspicious of the Young Ladies' Sodality.

A large new air compressor for the Erie mine in Graniteville arrived yesterday.

British troops occupy Johannesburg.

Memorial Day was observed in Nevada City with hundreds of people laden with flowers wending their way to the cemeteries.

Hot on the first, heavy showers mid-month, then more hot weather.

Tomorrow a number of local miners leave for Honolulu where they will be employed in a gravel mine.

The Illinois National Guard has purchased an automobile carriage with a Colt's machine gun mounted thereon. The vehicle can reach speeds nearing 35 miles per hour.

The infant child of Mr. and Mrs. William Trebilcox of Hills Flat died from convulsions.

The Grass Valley Stars will play a Wheatland baseball team at Watt Park.

Cavalry troops are in pursuit of a lone highwayman who held up five Yosemite stages.

Arrangements for the Fourth of July celebration progress nicely. It should be the grandest in the history of Grass Valley, a regular old time Fourth with cannon fire and bells greeting the sunrise.

A herd of 200 horses, up from Yuba City and destined to the mountains, passed through here.

Sandow, the famous strongman, helped to rescue two men in Paris who were almost crushed by a large bronze statue. Sandow held the statue up until help arrived.

Miss Dora Carver and Miss Kate Cozzens, representing the Western Mutual Investment Company, are in Grass Valley.

Susanville destroyed by fire. Forty buildings burned.

John Noonans, brought from Truckee for a mental examination, was declared crazy as a bedbug and will be taken to an asylum.

In the upcoming census, refusal to answer a question can result in a $100 fine.

In China, the Dowager Empress has thrown in her lot with the Boxers who threaten to kill all foreigners. Embassies in Peking are under siege.

John Biship was killed in Truckee while trying to couple a pair of freight cars. He was 62 and had been on the job only three days.

British marines landed in China. It's likely an international force will be necessary to relieve the embassies in Peking.

The city trustees found discrepancies in several accounts. City clerk Carr had a shortage of $410.

Martin Rafter has been retuned to his parents after a few days runaway trip to the Ridge.

Burt Alvord and the rest of his train robbery gang are holed up in the Arizona mountains, well supplied with horses, guns and ammunition provided by friendly cowboys. The bandits are negotiating with authorities over surrender terms.

The bicycle ordinance against riding on sidewalks was suspended for 90 days due to the poor conditions of the streets.

Death claimed James Hammell, one of the areas most competent miners, from consumption brought on by years of giant powder smoke.

Rifles and artillery were captured by U.S. troops in the Philippines.

William Grenfel and 'Spring' Curry, who brutally attacked a Chinese peddler, were fined $90 each.

Ed Conners of Nevada City has been causing a lot of trouble lately. He was escorted to Colfax and told to not return.

Sheriff Getchell received a picture of a man suspected of holding up the Yosemite stages and who was seen here not long ago.

The Japanese Government has notified the Treasury Department that it will restrain immigration of their subjects to the U.S.

In another I-didn't-know-the-gun-was-loaded case, a Spenceville sheepherder shot himself in the foot.

A Collector has said that original Confederate bank notes, stamps and bonds, slave deeds, etc. have about run out and counterfeits are now being made.

John Tin Loy's brand new rig was destroyed when the horse ran off through Chinatown, smashing the buggy.

The class of 1900 will bid adieu to school life at an evening program at the Methodist Church.

Local saloonkeepers can remain open after hours from July 4 through 6th—as long as arrests don't pick up.

Recent social dances at the Armory and the Union were successes.

Postmaster George's salary was increased $100 a year to $2300.

Four sailors were the first American fatalities in the fighting in China.

Thomas Torpie was on a rampage last night. He was full of liquor and will be seeing the judge.

A baby beauty contest will be held on the afternoon of the 4th—a cord of oak firewood will be the prize.

French Corral will host their own 4th celebration with sports and amusements topped off with fireworks and a grand ball.

Though resisting, Governor Roosevelt was placed on the ticket with McKinley by acclimation.

Thomas Berryman severely whipped young Thomas Harvey, a small lad he caught swimming in Berryman's pond. Berryman was fined $40.

A Smartsville miner named Davidson was drowned while rafting down the Yuba the other day.

Eve got Adam so cheap that women have been looking for bargains ever since.

FORBIDDEN GOLD

It Could Only Be Produced

By Destroying

by

Brad Prowse

Supported by thousands of miles of water flume and numerous dams built in the Sierra fastness, great cannons once washed down complete mountains in the California goldfields during the eighteen-hundreds. The resultant silting up of the riverbeds in the valley below caused widespread flooding. It was, arguably, America's first great ecological disaster.

The men who flocked to the California gold fields after James Marshall's initial discovery near Coloma in 1848 found the rumors true. Nuggets could be picked up right out of the streams and rivers...but not for long. As soon as this 'loose' gold was gone, the miners had to work hard for their treasure, using panning, various types of sluice box—long toms, cradles or rockers—and, finally, wresting the gold from the mountains by drilling into the quartz itself.

Today all these methods are still used by the miners—most recreational, a few serious—who still match wits with the mountains for its golden hoard. But there is one type of gold retrieval, once very popular and productive, that one won't see; hydraulic mining, the washing away of entire hillsides by using water cannons—monitors in mining parlance.

Sluice mining, where gold-bearing debris is washed down into a wooden box studded with gold-catching crosspieces, required great amounts of water. By 1852, elaborate ditches and flumeworks had been constructed to bring water from distant sources to wherever a promising sluice operation might be. About that same year, a Frenchman named Chabot, working a claim at Buckeye Hill, near Nevada City, California, made a canvas hose forty feet long and four or five inches in diameter. He used it to wash away earth that had become packed down near the sluicebox.

The following year, in April of 1853, E. E. Matteson, a Connecticut Yankee working a claim at American Hill, also near Nevada City, rigged up a hose like Chabot's. Only, Matteson attached some sort of nozzle to it and found that by directing the stream of water at a hillside, the work of a hundred men could be accomplished with water pressure alone. Within a short space of time, 'hydraulicking' came into favor throughout the mining country. It was practiced in such counties as Amador, Yuba, Placer and El Dorado but it was especially prevalent in Nevada County, most hydraulic diggings being not far from Nevada City, the county seat and an important gold town.

The most important element in developing a hydraulic diggings was water. In thirty years over 5000 miles of ditch and flumework would be built, fed by numerous dams constructed high up in the Sierra fastness. It was an engineering feat to rival the construction of the continental railroad. Where lakes were scarce, artificial lakes were built. Where water had to be routed around sheer cliffs, wooden flumes were built—or hard rock tunnels bored—to carry the water. The outlay represented an investment of around $20,000,000 with a like sum invested in equipment at the various diggings.

At the final destination the water might be fed to holding ponds above the diggings. Various pipelines—up to two feet in diameter and now made of riveted boiler iron, not canvas—would feed the water to the monitors.

Observers spoke in awe of the power of the water from a monitor. In his book, Gold Is The Corner Stone, John Walton Caughey writes, "...it literally ate into the hillside, undermining the higher part of the bank to bring it down in an immense slide, toppling stalwart trees and loosening tons of earth..."

The roar of a monitor, fed by perhaps a 600 foot drop of water, was said to be deafening. A monitor could discharge 1,570 cubic feet of water per minute or, in ten hours of operation, 7,085,000 gallons. Thrown two hundred feet at the base of a hill, it didn't take long to reduce it to flattened ground. It was said that a fifty pound boulder dropped into the stream would be carried a hundred feet before dropping out of its own weight.

The monitor, made of iron, was a goosenecked-shaped device that allowed the water to be directed wherever on a rise of ground it was desired to wash away earth. A box of stones at the back of the monitor counterbalanced the weight of the muzzle. The monitor could be swung sideways and raised or lowered by the operator. Monitors came in various sizes but the largest could run to ten inches at the muzzle.

The monitor was controlled by one man, using a system of deflection plates. According to W. W. Kallenberger, who, as a young man, worked at the famous Malakoff hydraulic diggings, twenty miles from Nevada City, it was a chance discovery that led to this novel method of controlling the monitors.

"...Dave Stokes, the foreman in the pit (was) cleaning his shovel by lacing the blade against the jet of water and noticed that the (monitor) by this slight deflection moved on its gooseneck..."

Using this knowledge, mine superintendent Henry Perkins got a patent on a deflector that, by its slightest movement, the monitor could be easily controlled. It paved the way for the huge monitors to come.

The debris brought down by the monitors was directed toward sluice boxes for processing, though in some cases, stamp mills were used to crush the rock. It was an inefficient way of mining—much gold was lost in the speedy race of the sluice box—and sometimes a second sluice was placed below the first with grate-work in the upper allowing the finer gold pieces to fall into the second, slower moving, sluice box.

Even at that, much gold was left in the final tailings. These were usually disdained by the hydraulickers and companies sprang up that contracted out to work these tailings, in some cases, recovering as much gold that way as was gleaned by the sluices that produced them.

It's been estimated that the first half billion dollars in gold taken from California was from placer mining. The second half billion was done by the hydraulickers. Hard rock mining took out the next billion. It's not hard to see why hydraulicking was so popular. For one thing, it wasn't labor intensive. Once the dams and ditches were built—and some separate company might construct these and sell the water to the hydraulic diggings—you needed only a row of monitors, one man on each, and you could work through an entire hill, reducing it to a veritable moonscape.

At the then-current pay of four dollars a day, it cost twenty dollars to process a cubic yard of earth by panning. Using a rocker reduced the cost to five dollars and a long tom, to one dollar. Hydraulicking cut the cost to twenty cents.

Hydraulic mining wasn't without its danger. Occasionally a bank being undermined would collapse forward without warning, covering the monitor and its operator. Kallenberger remembers a man named Cotton was trapped when a bank caved.

"None knew the exact spot where the body lay and it was up to the monitor to tear away the muck and uncover the body."

If hydraulicking had continued, it's possible that today the Sierra Nevadas would be washed featureless, leaving nothing but a smooth upslope from the flats of the Sacramento Valley to the slot machines of Reno—what a downhill run for the skiers! But other forces were at work—forces as strong as the water stream from a monitor.

Even before the hydraulickers the Sacramento Valley was subject to widespread floods. The valley is the meeting point for numerous large

152

rivers—the Sacramento, American, Yuba, Feather, Cosumnes, Mokelumne and Calaveras, among other tributaries. The reason that early settler John Sutter put his fort where he did in 1841—a mile or so from the Sacramento River—was because it was the highest spot around that neck of the woods.

In the early 1850s, well before hydraulicking, the booming town of Sacramento experienced devastating floods. So much so, that the town elected to fill in its buildings up to the first story, effectively raising the whole town by about eight feet. Even today archaeologists occasionally explore this 'buried' city to gather artifacts and knowledge of Gold Rush days.

The debris sent down the rivers by hydraulic mining started to fill the beds of these already flood-prone streams. The farmers and townspeople in the valley had to build levees to protect themselves from the ever-rising rivers. Navigation was impaired as far downstream as the Carquinez Straight, at the eastern end of San Francisco Bay. Given enough time, even the Golden Gate may have been effected. To this day, the valley still is subject to horrendously costly floods, all exacerbated by the hydraulic tailings of a hundred years ago.

Groups of valley people began to petition the legislature to do something about this filling in of the rivers and suit was brought on their behalf. The miners fought back, using the slogan' Live and Let Live,' but to no avail. In 1884, Judge Sawyer of the 9th Circuit Court issued an injunction against the hydraulickers. It didn't exactly ban the practice but it forbad anyone doing so from emptying their tailings into any navigable waterway—which virtually all foothill streams were regarded as.

The miners ignored the rule—for awhile. Some ran their operations at night, closing down during the day when the inspectors were likely to be around. Even modern technology came into play. What is sometimes called America's first long distance telephone line, from Smartsville to North Bloomfield, a distance of about twenty-five miles, was pressed into service. Lookouts stationed in Smarstville, about fifteen miles from the valley floor, would watch for men who looked like inspectors. If any were seen, they'd phone the Malakoff Diggings near North Bloom-field and warn them to shut down and look innocent.

And they built special damns to trap the debris, along with other methods, all of which were marginal and drove up the cost of operations. Finally, in 1892, Congress set up a commission to regulate hydraulic mining, requiring a permit to be issued prior to such mining work being done. The few operations struggling to keep going slowly folded and by the 1900s, hydraulicking had pretty much ground to a halt.

Besides the $40,000,000 invested in ditch/flumework, dams and equipment, it's estimated that the value of the mines themselves was in the neighborhood of $60,000,000—a fair purse in a day of gold legal tender and nickel bread. And in a time of robber barons, it might seem quite a victory of the 'little guy' over the corporate giants. But, in fact, the farmers and townspeople in the valley were a lot closer to the seats of power—the legislature in Sacramento—and were not without clout...or a war chest. And many mines were small and not all that able to spend huge amounts of money to fight the decision.

In the end, the Sawyer Decision wiped out an entire industry, negating all that invested capital and wiping out the fortunes of an entire industry. But not quite. It turned out that all those dams and miles of ditchwork could be put to another use. About this time the infant electric power business, just beginning to furnish electricity to the foothill towns and the hard-rock mines, needed water to spin their turbines and Pelton wheels. The ditches were quickly put to use to drive the water-wheels that generated electricity.

As it turned out, the little powerhouse on the South Fork of the Yuba River, not far from Nevada City, would prove to be the nucleus of a new company. From the ashes of the hydraulic mining industry sprang a new, even more profitable business—the giant corporation, the Pacific Gas and Electric Company—the main supplier of power to the State of California.

End

100 YEARS AGO IN NEVADA COUNTY

July, 1900

by

Brad Prowse

Nevada City will outdo itself Independence Day with parades, amusements, orations and fireworks.

Marshall Deeble said fireworks will not be permitted during the parade.

Weather hot. Showers on the 21st.

A disastrous fire in New York! Hundreds perish! $10,000,000 property loss!

The Washington Stage, driven by Henry Kohley, upset near Willow Valley. Damages to coach and passengers were relatively minor.

A skeleton found about three miles from Nevada City is thought to be either Charles Grady, who went missing some six years ago, or Wallace Bruce, who wandered away from the county hospital in 1888.

Boxers besiege embassies in Peking.

The Fourth in Grass Valley was celebrated with parades, athletic events a wild west show, fireworks and a dance.

Fred Brough swore out an arrest warrant against his brother—family problems.

Democrats nominate Bryant for president on a free silver ticket against imperialism and militarism.

Nevada County assessment rolls are up $70,000 over last year.

Oscar Reynolds of Newtown brought in a pelican killed near Deer Creek.

San Francisco is considering tapping into the Yuba River to supply the city. Engineer, W. F. Englebright proposes to place a dam near Alabama Bar. Supervisor Reid claimed that if Yuba water was secured, the City would have all the power and water it needs at virtually no cost.

An explosion at the Home mine two miles from Nevada City badly injured three miners.

Talks about arming the National Guard with the new Krag-Jorgensen rifles are being held in Sacramento. The old Springfields are badly outclassed by the modern, high speed bullets from the Mausers used by the Insurrectos.

155

Deer season starts soon. Reports are that a buck was taken by hunters near Central House. They better be careful.

Those attending the theater last night to see the Mellville Vaudeville Company were pleased with the performance.

Word from the embassies in Peking indicates the situation is desperate.

The Nevada City band will soon have new uniforms.

Former Grass Valley resident Ed Burns was arrested in Auburn for stealing a pair of shoes.

A plot to assassinate President McKinley by a group of Spanish and Cuban conspirators has been uncovered.

Two play houses, one for boys, one for girls, are being erected on the Washington school grounds.

It's expected the ledge in the Anglo-Saxon mine will soon be reached via tunneling and a mill may be built.

A three foot, nine inch rattlesnake was killed Sunday near Round Mountain by Ralph Maitland.

Hundreds of Mojave Indians mill about Needles, agitated over the Superintendent's decision to make the children work the Indian school's farm instead of going home for the summer.

Edger Clinton of Rock Creek succumbed to consumption.

The new court house clock will weigh around 2000 pounds and cost $750.

There was considerable anxiety in town yesterday by those dependent on electricity as a power plant accident shut down the system for awhile.

Terrible explosion in Nevada City when George Turner's powder magazine blew up last night. The report was heard for miles away. Fifteen tons of powder were situated above the Reward Mine about three-quarters of a mile south-west of town. Damage in town was confined mainly to broken storefront windows.

The Jamestown Chinese quarters were nearly burned out.

A jolly crowd gathered at the Van Slyke's ranch for the Grass Valley Sportsmen's annual buck stew.

William Fair, arrested for bigamy, was released due to lack of evidence.

R. Paine of Lake City, driving a heavy six-team load, had a brake fail, resulting in an injured horse that had to be destroyed.

Some young boys are in the habit of donning grotesque masks at night and frightening ladies. Marshall Deeble said arrests will be made if the practice continues.

George Ryan, a telephone lineman, came into contact with a power line and fell to the ground, seriously injured.

Word from China says the embassies there are being bombarded daily and are dangerously short of ammunition. The threat of massacre is imminent. Troops gathered from all the principal nations of the world are rushing to their aid.

Two masked men with pistols raided a Truckee saloon, robbing the faro bank of $100. They then rode off in a carriage.

There are only three men on the chain gang at present, breaking rock on the Gold Flat dump.

Eighty natives killed by U.S. troops in the Philippines after an American soldier was found beheaded.

Grass Valley was swept by a tremendous conflagration. Loss set at $125,000. The most disastrous fire since 1855, it started at a laundry in the Glasson Building. A greater part of two blocks along Main Street are gone. No lives were lost.

Did you hear about Mr. Titewadd's wife? She said she would kill herself if he didn't buy her a new bonnet.

No! What happened?

Titewadd got several estimates on funerals, decided a new hat was cheaper and saved her life.

Early-day Graniteville

The Golden State Hotel was the place Monkey went to get help

MONKEY SHINES

by

Brad Prowse

The horse: Not an animal that thinks or has any real intelligence; not an animal that acts but one that only reacts. Well, maybe... but then, how do you explain the little sorrel gelding named Monkey?

In 1900, Graniteville was a small but thriving gold town nestled in the high Sierras about 100 miles north-east of Sacramento. Besides the town itself, there were nearby gold mines and several sawmills to cut and process the local timber, mainly pine, Douglas fir and cedar.

One of these mills was owned by a man by the name of Smart who was busy working on a contract to furnish 200,000 board feet of lumber for water flumes. These flumes would be used to supply water to the hydraulic diggins near another Sierra gold town, originally named Humbug but now called North Bloomfield.

Smart's mill was closed down one weekend in 1901—his crew off to town—so he was there all alone when he discovered a fire in one of his buildings. Smart immediately began to fight the fire with whatever means were at hand. As he did so, his little sorrel gelding, Monkey, ran up to him, obviously agitated but seemingly more anxious to help Smart than to run away.

Smart quickly wrote a note, tied it into Monkey's mane and sent him on down the road toward Graniteville, several miles away. When he got there, the little horse dashed down the main street of the town and up the steps of the Golden State Hotel. Part way up the steps he was met by Willy McCleen, who spotted the note tied in the horse's mane.

McCleen quickly read the note, a message outlining the problem and pleading for help. Within a short time Smart, frantically fighting the flames, looked up to see a band of townsfolk thundering up the road toward the mill with Monkey, now saddled and carrying a rider, in the lead.

The fire was quickly brought under control. Smart suggested they all retire to the nearby dining hall where Monkey was brought in and feted with a hearty meal. Then Smart suggested they hold a dance and a party was made out of what—without the little horse, Monkey—could have been a financial calamity. And Smart vowed that from then on, Monkey would only be ridden on special occasions. The little horse had earned an early retirement.

Dumb animals?

END

Sheriff Douglass

THE STRANGE CASE OF
SHERIFF DOUGLASS

1896-1962

by

Brad Prowse

In 1961, the sheriff of Nevada County, California received a phone call from a private attorney in Sacramento. It seemed that one of the attorney's clients had disclosed to him that the client's former father-in-law had confessed to the killing of a man in that county. The man was apparently trying to cause problems for his ex-wife's father. In any case, the information was being offered.

Sheriff Wayne Brown played around with the papers on his desk for a few seconds, racking his brain to fit some circumstances to the man's words. Finally he had to admit that there weren't any bodies laying about in the Nevada County morgue awaiting a suspect to fit their demise. Could the attorney be a little more specific? Who was killed...and when?

The answer, when it came forth, stunned the Nevada County man. The victim was Nevada County Sheriff David Douglass who was gunned down on the 26th of July...in 1896.

When dark deeds of the Old West are mentioned—gunfights, stage holdups, road agentry and the like—people usually think of the `cowboy' states such as Wyoming, Montana, Texas and Arizona. In truth, California can generally match any of them for daring outlaws, badmen and all-around scoundrels and it can lay claim to them over a longer period of time. California, thanks to the Gold Rush, found itself peopled early on by an undisciplined and rowdy crowd of young men who were no strangers to the feel of a Colt revolver. As early as 1850, when a lot of other `western' territories were still largely peopled by Indians and Mountain Men, California was gaily shooting, stabbing, robbing and—subsequently— hanging men at a rate to put those other areas to shame. Furthermore, she was still providing stage and train robbers well into the twentieth century.

A lot of this had to do with the remoteness of a good portion of California's gold country. While towns dotted the slopes of the Sierra and the telephone and even the electric light were not unknown by the 1890s, there was still a lot of distance between the different camps and many a place for a man who didn't want to be found to not be found. This, plus the plentiful outpouring of the mines, mostly hard rock by now, made it easy and lucrative to be a highwayman. Travelers would usually be carrying at least some money and disappearing into the fastness of the mountains was fairly easy. And in the summer of 1896, an enterprising gentleman of the byways decided to take advantage of the Sierra's bounty.

On July 14th, Thomas Gibson—a San Francisco detective, of all things—and a friend, Charles Sladky, had their buggy stopped by a lone gunman three miles north of Nevada City. Waving a repeating rifle, he convinced the two men to divest themselves of their valuables. The detective's friend tried to argue that his watch, a keepsake, should not be included in the haul. While the detective, taking up the cudgel for Sladky, argued the fine points of sentiment vs. outlawry, a second vehicle approached. The bandit bade Gibson and Sladky to move on, the latter, interestingly enough, still clutching his watch.

The second buggy was stopped but the two men in it managed to stiff the outlaw—they were broke. These two were waved on also and the bandit disappeared into the brush, ninety dollars richer for his efforts. Meanwhile, Gibson rode into Nevada City and sounded the alarm. And this brings Sheriff Douglass into the story.

Sheriff David Fulton Douglass was a handsome man. He was described as being above average in height with a thin, wiry build. The old pictures show a good head of hair, nicely swept up into a wave in front and a full, wide mustache, tightly curled at the ends. He was a native Californian and had worked at cattle raising in Nevada and farming in California before taking up a shotgun to work as a Wells-Fargo messenger. Later he fulfilled the same office for a narrow gauge railroad in California's Sierra-Nevada Mountains.

In 1890, when he was 32, Douglass was appointed under-sheriff by Sheriff Pascoe of Nevada County, nominally serving out of the county seat in Nevada City, 50 miles north-east of Sacramento. But Pascoe was killed in a shooting in 1893 and Douglass was appointed to serve out his term by the board of supervisors. In 1894, Douglass ran for election as sheriff in his own right. After the votes were counted Douglass wore the star, fairly won, of Sheriff of Nevada County, California. So, when the detective, Gibson, rode in and reported the holdup, it was Sheriff Douglass' job to catch him.

In the days before fingerprints, blood types and instant communication between law enforcement agencies, police work often devolved down to nothing more than a lot of legwork—riding about and looking, watching for strangers, talking to people. (Actually, not too much different from what a lot of police work still involves to get a case solved, despite all the modern crime solving gifts of science.) In any case, there wasn't much physical evidence at the scene of the crime, just some dusty footprints leading off into the brush and disappearing in the pine needles and manzanita leaves.

The sheriff did have a pretty good description of the man, however, as he hadn't worn a mask. He was about 5 foot 7, 150 to 160 pounds, had brown hair, blue eyes and a sandy mustache. His clothes were common. He wore a striped shirt and brown overalls, a white hat and vest but no coat. Later that day, Douglass learned that another man was held up a few miles from the first robbery site. The bandit got $31, called the man—Joe Waters—by name and tossed back 50 cents to him "…because he didn't like to see a man broke."

It might seem, considering the small sums relieved from the travelers, $90 in one case, $31 in another, that Sheriff Douglass really didn't have much of a crime wave on his hand. But it must be taken into account that $30 was a good month's wages in 1896. If you compare that to a man making, say, $10 an hour today, that would equate out to around $1700. Furthermore, anytime a road agent goes around waving a Winchester in people's faces, there's a chance of someone getting killed. And, a law officer in those times considered his bailiwick in a much more possessive vein than might be usual today. There was a bandit operating on Sheriff Douglass' turf and he took that personal!

There were other considerations too. As the bandit struck again and again, local newspapers began to put the heat on Douglass.

Three days after the initial holdup William Engle was driving a four-team freight wagon along the dusty Lake City Road, about thirteen miles from Nevada City. The road along here is lined with scrub oaks, small pines and manzanita bushes, natural habitat for a road agent. When he first saw the man, Engle thought he might be a laborer heading for the diggings at North Bloomfield. He realized his mistake when the .38 revolver appeared.

"Throw out your money, and be damned quick about it!" the bandit shouted. The driver threw out to the tune of $14. Again, the bandit wore no mask and again he matched the description from the first holdup.

Douglass sent out Deputy Neagle with a bloodhound, 'Jim Budd,' but by the time they got to the scene of the robbery, too many others had been there for the dog to sort out a good scent.

On the 18th, Walter Selpar, a vegetable peddler traveling along the Lake City road, found himself looking down the barrel of a revolver. The view cost him $30.

The newspaper continued to put pressure on Douglass. He spent more and more of his time riding out into the county, talking to farmers, ranchers and miners, looking into the face of every stranger he ran across and warning people to be on the lookout for any suspicious men. But even though the road agent always managed to elude him, bits and pieces of information began to dribble in.

Henry Kirtchberger, a miner living near the old Nevada City Mine, reported that two men had tried to break into his cabin one night. He discouraged them with a shotgun, though they hung around awhile, out of range. One carried a rifle while the other had a revolver. This information fit in with talk beginning to go around that the bandit might have an accomplice. A Chinese fruit peddler told Constable Loehr that before the Gibson holdup he'd seen the man that later proved out to be the bandit on the road with a second man. The peddler had stopped and talked with them. And the collection of unauthorized road tolls continued.

Max Isoard claimed he had been commanded to "Throw out your money!" Always ready for a fight, Max threw out a .38 instead but the bandit's gun was faster and Max, seeing the man had the drop on him, turned over his pistol. If it was any consolation to Max, he was lucky to keep his life.

Not all the highwayman's attempts were successful. A salesman riding near French Corral, twenty miles from Nevada City, was ordered to stop. The youth riding with the drummer suddenly applied the whip to the horse. While the disappointed bandit looked on, the buggy, peddler and boy went careening down the road, unscathed.

William Berry was held up on the 25th and a farmer reported that earlier in the month he had had a shotgun stolen by a drifter who'd stayed overnight. The man then went to the next farm and, when no one was looking, swapped the shotgun for a rifle.

Again on the 25th, the same day Berry was held up, Sheriff Douglass was riding around the Wells Milk Ranch, a few miles north of Nevada City. He had tied his horse and was scouting around on foot when he spotted a man he felt might be the bandit. The man began to run and Douglass, his horse too far away, ran to a nearby road and commandeered a mount from a passerby. Astride, Douglass gave chase. At one point he fired at the fleeing man but missed and soon lost him in the dense underbrush.

Douglass returned to Nevada City but the next day he went to a local stable and had his horse hitched to a buggy. He'd received word from Miss Della Wells of the Wells Milk Ranch that footprints had been seen near a local spring. This led him to believe that the bandit—or bandits—were making camp somewhere in the area of Sugar Loaf Hill, not far from the milk ranch. As Douglass left town, 'Jack,' a dog that belonged to a friend, tagged along after him. The dog returned later that afternoon, around four o'clock...alone.

Deputy William Pascoe, the son of the sheriff slain in 1893, grew worried about the sheriff's failure to return. Early the next morning, a Monday, he left to search for Douglass. Later that same morning H.D. Towle came into town to report that a horse and buggy had been tied near his place since the previous afternoon. Two deputies, James Neagle and Martin McGrath, left for Towle's place near Sugar Loaf Hill, about two miles outside of town.

They found the horse and buggy and soon located two sets of footprints that they could see Douglass had been tracking. They followed the footprints until McGrath, in the lead, came upon the body of a man who lay face up, eyes closed, with his coat folded neatly and placed under his head. Nearby lie a Winchester rifle. He dismounted and drew his pistol as the man—at first—looked to be sleeping. Then he saw another figure on the ground. It was Sheriff Douglass. Both men were dead.

In piecing together what had happened—as close as anyone could determine—the death of Sheriff Douglass came about like this.

Douglass drove to the top of Sugar Loaf Hill where he tied his horse. He searched around until he found the tracks of two men walking along the dusty road. Recognizing them as being fresh, Douglass started following them on foot, letting them lead him into the thickets of pine and cedar trees and brush covering the area around Sugar Loaf Hill. Pistol in hand, a long-barreled Colt's .44, he worked his way to a small clearing about 150 feet across. Stepping into the clearing, he pulled down on a man holding a Winchester rifle, calling out for him to lay aside his gun.

The man moved suddenly, the rifle swinging around toward the sheriff and Douglass fired, close enough to the man to leave powder burns on his clothes. The gun bucking in his hand, he thumbed off one or two more shots and the bandit, hit twice, fell, mortally wounded. (The shots didn't go unnoticed. A Mr. Dean, who lived nearby, heard the pistol shots, close together. Then, a short space of time later, a louder, much stronger report— like that from a rifle.)

Douglass must have stood there a moment, the smoke from his gun hanging before him in the still, July air. Then, from about 30 feet away, someone with a .44 rifle—down slope, from the angle of the wounds in the sheriff's body—shot the sheriff twice, killing him.

It's possible that the third man had no idea that Douglass was a sheriff until after he'd shot him. Uniforms weren't common at the time and since Douglass was hit from the back, his badge may not have been noticed until after he fell, and maybe not then—the sheriff was laying face down. It may have been that the sheriff's killer thought that Douglass was another bandit or just an ordinary citizen who'd stumbled across their camp.

The killer had taken the time to go through the pockets of the dead men. Before he left he apparently folded the outlaw's coat and put it under his head and placed the dead man's hands across his chest, 'mortician style.' No such final offices were performed for the sheriff. Since one of Douglass' bullets had gone through the bandit's heart, it was unlikely he had lived for more that a few seconds after Douglass had shot him. This 'third man' then fled. The only traces of him were a few .44 cases left on the ground.

An expert tracker was sent for in the hopes he might be able to pick up the trail of the third man, but he had no success. A cordon was thrown around the area and suspects questioned, but nothing positive was turned up. When the body of the bandit was displayed in town, several people recognized him as a man they knew, by the name 'C. Meyers,' who had worked at a local sawmill some months before. They recalled that he often bummed meals from people in the area and often asked, after eating, for a 'lunch' to be eaten later. It seemed likely this was for his unknown companion.

Sheriff Douglass received a well attended funeral and proper burial in a local cemetery. The bandit, Meyers, was buried in an unmarked grave. Later, monuments were erected at the location of the shootings where they still can be seen. As time went by, the third man was slowly forgotten...for 66 years.

In 1961, certain Nevada County officials, principally Sheriff Wayne Brown and District Attorney Harold Berliner, were contacted by the Sacramento attorney. He related a tale told to him by a client from Oregon about the client's former father-in-law. One time, under the influence of alcohol, the old man had admitted to his wife that he had killed a sheriff in California when he was a boy. The ex-son-in-law learned of this—possibly from his former wife—and was willing to finger the old man for spite. Brown and the district attorney launched an investigation into the matter. After over a year of sifting through old records, attempting to trace the movements of the boy, 12 or 13 years old at the time, and conferring with the Sacramento attorney, the following story was finally put together.

Just how the boy and the bandit, Meyers, came to become partners is not known. But the boy was indeed the 'third man' at the scene of the shooting upon whom so much time and trouble to locate was spent after the sheriff's death. But because he was a young boy, he was not suspected. He went into Nevada City but soon fled the area as soon as he was able and made it to Marysville, 30 miles away in the Sacramento Valley. There he was briefly questioned and then released. (There is one story that during the autopsy on Douglass by Doctor Alfred Trickell, a boy of about 12 years, hiding in the shadows of the room, cried out in terror. Trickell tossed him out into the hallway.)

The boy then made his way to Colorado where he worked as a miner before moving on to Oklahoma. Later, he moved into the Washington-Oregon area where he joined a nationwide company as a salesman and moved up through the ranks to become manager of the Portland office. He married, reared a family and was, at the time of his retirement, a man of some wealth.

Further statements attributed to the old man—now in his 80s—were that in later years he considered searching for Sheriff Douglass' son to confer a sum of money on him. It was not determined if he ever tried to do so. Another time the man was supposed to have said, "I had to shoot him (Douglass). It was him or me."

This last statement illuminates a sidelight to the affair, implied but never directly brought out. It may well have been that the boy could, physically, have passed for a young man. This is inferred by the fact that, in the aftermath of the death of Douglass and Meyers, people had remembered seeing Meyers with another 'man,' the third man all were looking for. Also, if one set of the footprints that Douglass had been following was smaller than the other, somebody probably would have noticed it and made mention of the fact.

And if the boy was only around 13 years old when questioned in Marysville, why wasn't he detained, if he was on his own? It would have been likely, if he was of such tender years, that he would have been placed in the proper facilities as was common to do for runaways and orphans at the time…unless his appearance was that of an older boy, say sixteen or so.

Lastly, if the boy felt that "…it was him or me." when it came to the choice of surrendering to Douglass or killing him, then it might have been because it wasn't obvious that he was a mere boy, who the sheriff would have been unlikely to shoot, even if he had been armed. If he indeed appeared older than his years, Douglass might very well—in the heat of a battle he had just fought—have shot a boy who suddenly appeared and looked to be fully grown and was armed with a rifle. It may have been, in fact, almost an act of self-defense on the part of the boy when he killed the sheriff.

The thing that might refute this argument is the fact that Douglass was shot in the back. Still, the boy may have felt he had no choice. A 13 year-old, no matter how large physically, would still be working with the reasoning of a 13 year old. To him, it may have been all he could think of to do to save himself.

After going over all the pertinent information, it was the decision of the Nevada County district attorney to not pursue the matter. For one thing, there were no witnesses to the killings and the old man, if brought before the bar, could just deny everything. There would be no one to stand witness against him. Further, had he been brought to trial at the time of the actual killing, due to his tender years he'd probably have been put in a reform school until he'd reached maturity and then released.

It was decided that little would be gained in trying to extradite and try an 80 year old man for a crime that few still living would even have remembered. But Sheriff Brown was enough satisfied with the evidence to finally mark the case of the killing of Sheriff Douglass `closed,' 66 years after it occurred.

END

ABOUT THE AUTHOR

I was born in Hayward, California in 1935 and graduated – by Act of Congress – from high school there. I served a stint with the U.S. Post Office; I still have the dog-bite marks and then three years with Uncle Sammy in the Far East as a GI. Finally, after a few years working at a Bay Area electronics firm, I moved to Nevada County following a short stay in Colorado/Montana.

I raised two children and became a grass widower, because she got smart and moved away to Alaska! I toiled in the clutches of an electronic firm, the Grass Valley Group, for twenty-four years actually, a pleasant place to work until the final year.

Since then I have been semi-retired, writing, riding my horse in the Sierra foothills, and hopelessly spoiling my five grandchildren and blaming their resultant bad behavior on their parents.